Teachable
Moments

Teachable *Moments*

Practice Run for the Rest of Your Life

Linda Gibson Fletcher, PhD

TEACHABLE MOMENTS

The information provided within this book is for general informational and educational purposes only. The author does not guarantee results and makes no representations or warranties, express or implied, about the completeness, accuracy, reliability, suitability or availability with respect to the information, products, services, or related graphics contained in this book for any purpose. Any use of this information is at your own risk.

Teachable Moments: Practice Run for the Rest of Your Life © 2021 by Linda Gibson Fletcher, PhD.
Cover Design by Jose Pepito Jr.
Edited by Diana Smith
Interior Design by Jose Pepito Jr.

Paperback ISBN: 978-1-7360303-5-6
eBook ISBN: 978-1-7360303-6-3
Printed in The United States of America

1st Edition / 2021

To my village that has kept me
close and poured out love

Contents

Part III
LIFE LESSONS

Part IV
TESTIMONIES

Author's Note

Life always presents strange twists. While I captured notes on teachable moments as a keepsake for my sons, they gifted me with a book of 20 lessons from their journey in life with me, for a total of 60 lessons. The gift they handed me turned into a journey with my sons' writings: my reactions and reflections to their thoughts, lessons they learned, and words I wish had and hadn't landed on the pages. I found myself birthing "Teachable Moments." The urgency to write became essential during a pandemic, racial unrest, the questions of truth and democracy, and the unexpected.

What have I learned?

Many days while parenting, I stopped and said, "This is a Teachable Moment! Stop what you are doing and listen. I am going to tell you something you need to hear, something you really cannot live without."

I have learned that life is a journey. The walk consists of turns, dips, sunshine, slides, slips, hurricanes, floods, and twists, and it happens in every stage of life. It appears that turns or drops only occur for you or me but be confident in knowing everyone has the experience. Understand, no one escapes the journey. The great relief is there is always an estimated time of arrival to your destination. The time in life you are in will not last forever. Being in the valley prepares you for mountain top experiences. Learning lessons early in your life will help you manage yourself, your emotions, and obstacles in the depths of the valley without feeling hopeless and helpless.

Living in your teens is different from living in your 20s, 30s, the 40s, 50s or 60s. Each step requires a certain level of skills and learned lessons, or that period can seem to last forever with no end in sight. You will not always be on the mountain or in the valley. You will not cry or weep forever; neither will you shout for joy. Life is continually changing. Preparation is the only key to mastering what lies ahead.

Failure is a stepping stone to greatness and wisdom. The earlier you get comfortable with losses in your life, the easier you can accept wins. Then, challenges may seem more comfortable and reduce your fear of risks and opportunities. The price you pay is directly related to your willingness to learn. When children learn principles, problem-solving techniques, and places to ask questions or seek wise counsel, they can better control the pain of trials and tribulations. The tests will still come, but acquiring the skills necessary to manage their emotions, understanding their values, and remembering the tools for the job, will help them think strategically (instead of emotionally) and weigh the cost of every decision before taking a step.

Introduction

THE CUMULATIVE FOLDER

When I was in high school, I had a chance to read my cumulative folder. A cumulative folder is a handwritten copy of all your final grades from Kindergarten through the 12ᵗʰ grade that follows you throughout your entire educational journey. As I read the comments posted and looked at my previous report grades, I encountered a very heartbreaking note. My second-grade teacher, Mrs. Struna, wrote, "Her mother's hopes are far too high for her."

I reread it and shocked by the comments, I started to cry. I wondered why Mrs. Struna wrote such a hopeless comment about me. I liked her as my teacher, but now her thoughts and views limited my hopes, dreams, and possibly my potential to grow. She disregarded and diminished what my mom had seen in me.

Why didn't Ms. Struna want to push me and help me become what my mom saw?

As a student, I behaved well in school. I earned good grades. Every day, I completed my work, participated in class, played kickball, baseball, and performed in all the school plays. I was also a brownie and a girl scout, I sang in the school and church choir, and volunteered in the community. Still, Miss Struna wrote, "Her mom's hopes are too high."

Those comments weren't on the report cards, and my mom didn't know to ask for the cumulative folder.

I never forgot the day I opened and read my cumulative folder. I never forgot how I felt and what I thought Ms. Struna felt about me. The cumulative folder incident became like a dagger in my heart. This once confident little girl now questioned everything about herself, who she was, and who she would even become. Why was this event so critical for me to experience at such an early age? I learned the power of a person's words. The comments on a piece of paper made me reflect on my life and myself. The teachers were friendly to me, always available to help me, but now I knew it was a lie. They didn't care. Their actions were much different than what they thought about me. From that moment, I prepared and equipped myself with information to help kids and teachers.

As a teacher, a principal, and a superintendent, I read the cumulative folders. I had the power to review the written words and correct any messages that didn't provide hope. I showcased the students' cumulative folders. I brought the folder out and cautioned kids to be mindful of their behavior and grades. I shared that teachers would write things on the lines that would follow them all the days of their life. I wanted them to know that the stroke of a pen and the strike on the computer keys could challenge their existence, creating a view of them that could go undisputed because they were unaware of the cumulative folder. I told them to make sure they presented themselves to teachers and counselors in order to receive only positive notes. I wanted kids and teachers to be aware that the folder should reflect hard work and unlimited potential.

Just think for one minute if Ms. Struna wrote these words: "Linda's mom has high expectations for her. Challenge her to be great. You will have her mother's full support."

I wonder where and what I would be today if one teacher believed in my greatness. Thank G-d for sending the first African-American administrator, Dr. Pat Ackerman Sneed, to my high school as the new assistant principal. She met me, loved me, made me her student assistant, and helped me explore my world and understand the unlimited possibilities which awaited me. Dr. Ackerman spoke unapologetically and sometimes her words pierced my ears. You would never catch her tongue-tied or mixing up her words. When she spoke, everyone listened. She modeled strength of character and greatness. I saw in her what I could become and more. She helped me see the necessity of holding my head up high and being somebody.

These lessons are necessary. If we don't spend the time providing a safe space for our kids to talk and be heard freely, someone in the streets will gladly put their arms around your child, listen to them, show them they care, and potentially take them away and destroy the essence of who they are and who they can become.

I pray that you receive some nuggets to chew on and use to advance your life and the people in your circle. I hope this lands in a place where you can say, "Right in the nick of time."

JOURNEY

One summer day, I packed up and drove down Interstate 75-Ohio to the University of Dayton to take my comprehensive exams for the last time. As I was driving, feeling overwhelmed and scared, I started to weep! I thought about the energy, expense, and price paid for me to even consider achieving an advanced degree. I thought not just about the trip I was taking but the journey of those before me.

Our journeys, what we experience and learn, are not just for our development and growth but also for the support we can give to others. We cannot assume that everyone knows. My stories will be an excellent example of not knowing, coming to an understanding, and sharing my newfound lessons. Since we are still here, our time is not up, and our work is not over! We still have time to get it right or to be better than we have ever been before.

THE AWAKENING

My mother was a maverick of her days, a first-generation college student in her family. Although she attended every homecoming or reunion in North Carolina, my mother never talked about her college experience or what campus life would be like for us. We visited the families who went to school with her, but we did not see the campus or talk about attending her college. Even as I think about my life in the church, I never knew there were teachers, professors, nurses, business owners, and entrepreneurs until I left for college and came home for visits. I wondered what people did, but nobody said a word. Even in our house, we knew we were going to college. It was not an option.

I guess that was one of the reasons we didn't talk about it. There was nothing to talk about, and it could have seemed senseless to my mom.

Just think if those men and women talked to each of us about college. Just suppose they conducted an annual workshop on finding a career for all the children in my church. It would have helped many who did not go to college. Just think of the power the church had to make each child richer and the community better. No one took us on a college tour or discussed various colleges in the area. There was no career day, absolutely nothing about how to accelerate your life and become better.

When I was getting my degree in 2002, there was one African-American man, Dr. Larry Little, attending a different institution to achieve the same goal. He was very instrumental in walking me through the process, standing by my side, encouraging me, and coaching me to succeed. It was his unwavering support that kept me focused and able to meet my goal. He coached, probed, and caused me to go deeper in my thinking, to develop a bigger picture embedded in my research. He was the only person I knew who had even attempted a doctorate. He let me in his world and helped me understand what was not only foreign to me but unknown in my circle. Later I asked him why. He shared that if he helped me, then more children would benefit. Teachers and administrators would be more successful, and ultimately, a community would thrive. He knew the knowledge would trickle to so many others, and he was right. Dr. Little demonstrated why coaching is essential. He coached and helped me orchestrate my steps to win. As an educator, I am always asking students what college they would like to attend, what they want to become, and what they would like to do. Anything to grab ahold of, to guide them in the direction of their dreams.

This journey we are about to embark on together is very similar. We are going to talk about how to improve what we do. Not because I am perfect, but because I have learned some lessons that might help you. I know each of you desires to be more prosperous today than yesterday, not only for yourself but for your children. Everything you need to begin this journey lies within. You have the fortitude and strength to make a difference with the big and little people in your family and circle of life.

I challenge you to think differently about being a parent. Challenge yourself as a provider and as the person who will coach your family to practice these necessary lessons and soft skills all the days they have an opportunity to be with you. I agree it is hard to think beyond being a parent because you do that with diligence and purpose. But think if you could add a little extra boost to the life of your kids, wouldn't you want to? When we become parents, we don't always weigh the cost of the job. It is a big job, a never-ending job! As a parent, you start with a baby, then a toddler, school-ager, teenager, young adults, grandkids, neighborhood kids, nieces, nephews, co-workers' kids, church family kids, and recreation center kids. The work-family gets more prominent as you move in different circles. But at every stage, there are lessons to be learned to help a child maneuver the course of life.

We think about food, clothes, shelter, and possibly college or trade school for each child. We rarely think about what inner strength is needed to exist in this world. We complete wills, insurance, and financial packages. We may even set up college plans, but rarely do we sit and craft teachings needed for character, purpose, and strength. Today, I ask that you explore this opportunity to teach these life lessons and skills for the journey ahead so you can keep, protect, and guide your loved ones.

The list of lessons is not exhaustive by any means. There may be a need for variations in some lessons based on where you live, or the family traditions historically embedded in your family's life. I am asking that you do not let life lessons happen by chance. Life is funny. It looks for weaknesses in the foundation, so corruption can enter—anything to break you. Life seeks to find out what is in your foundation. Is it as solid as a rock, or is it like sinking sand? What you build must have a solid foundation formed with an unbreakable and immovable rock.

Explore this opportunity to teach these life lessons and skills for the journey ahead to keep, protect, and guide your loved ones. We are preparing our family members to live in a community. We don't live outside of people. If we get this right with our family, they will get it right with theirs, and the whole community gets right.

HOW DO YOU PLANT?

"Train up a child in the way he should go: and when he is old, he will not depart from it."
Proverbs 22:6

"I am the vine; you are the branches. If a man remains in me and I in him, he will bear much fruit; apart from me, you can do nothing."
John 15:5

I planted a grapevine in 2012. When I planted the grapevine from Big Lots, I did not see a bit of evidence that the seedling took root.

A friend said, "It won't be this year."

But I planted it in good soil. I watered and weeded. I could not believe that I would not see the evidence of my planting. I saw sprouts in days from the seeds for my cucumbers, watermelons, and green beans. But that grapevine from Big Lots - nothing. I had to investigate why.

I found that growth depends on several environmental factors, such as how the plant is cared for, the sunlight, soil, and the proper pruning. These factors were necessary for plants to grow. Without a healthy root system, there would not be any grapes. Additionally, I found out the more sun you have, the sweeter the grapes. Finally, the grapes grew after 3 weeks...that the more sun you have, the sweeter the grapes.

When I was finally ready to get rid of it, it would not die! I chopped...*It would not die!* I chopped it, sprayed it, and covered it up. I dug deep in the ground and even removed it, and it lived. I looked outside, and again I saw the big, beautiful leaves of my grapevine.

If I liken this information to our children, it is essential to plant seeds to grow a healthy root system. Our children have at least 17-18 years with us. If we are granted that amount of time with our children, we can build a multifaceted and robust root system. If we create a healthy root system, our kids will be strong emotionally, spiritually, educationally, and physically. Then we will have sweet and valuable fruit hanging from the branches. The pages ahead are about developing the root system and what it takes to grow good fruit. None of this is a guarantee, but you are sure to lose and harvest some bad fruit without it.

FOUR ENVIRONMENTAL FACTORS MUST BE IN PLACE #1- CARE

Often, we find ourselves in a place where we think we are alone. I belong to a community, a village of family and friends. I am blessed to be surrounded by childhood and college friends who keep me centered and focused on what is essential and what matters at the end of a day. Most importantly, I have a Father in heaven who I have depended on all my life. I cannot think of one moment in my existence that I have not counted on or needed Him to help me be better, change an action, open a door, give me an idea, or help with the correct comment to change a heart.

As you read these chapters, consider your role and responsibility as a parent, grandparent, guardian, teacher, or responsible community member. You have an essential calling to teach and encourage boys and girls to be their best. This book contains teachable moments I have experienced with my boys throughout their lives. I attempted to clarify what is right and wrong and the reality of mishaps, misfortunes, and successes. I did not describe this world or myself as perfect. I tried desperately to make sure my children knew the love of our Father in heaven was the only reason for who I am and what I have been able to do for them and myself. He has given me everything. I cannot think of one accomplishment I have achieved on my own.

I also opened myself for examination and correction without penalty. I wanted my boys to know that I was and still am not perfect. If they are allowed to be parents, then they should change anything inappropriate or that hampered them from becoming all they should be or could be as future parents. I let them know that they could teach me at any time. They could discuss my wrongs so I could become better at parenting and providing for them.

One crucial principle to teach in your primetime moments is building your foundation on love and respect. Ruby Payne made an essential point in her book *A Framework for Understanding Poverty*. She states, "Poverty is thought of in terms of financial resources only. However, while fundamental, the reality is that financial resources do not explain the differences in the success with which individuals leave poverty nor the reason that many stay in poverty" (pg.16-17). I contend that what helps stabilize and even propel our success is the consistent spiritual commitment and family foundation as well as our relationships. Healthy relationships support your framework. Relationships are sustained when someone cares for you and holds you accountable for who you are in the relationship.

Your human resources are not exchangeable for giving yourself to your family and others. We need each other, and it is difficult, nearly impossible to exist without a community of people surrounding you with love. Show your kids and others how much you care about their existence. We show them by what we do and not what we say.

My mom used to say, "Don't do as I do. Do what I say."

What kind of sense does that make? The lesson is hypocritical. When actions and words don't match, it is hard to trust and take someone seriously. Tomorrow they might change their mind based on the circumstances they find themselves in. Some young adults know they cannot count on some of their friends or parents. If they say they will show up, it is a 50/50 chance. When you care for someone, you want to make sure they can trust you. Truth should line up to your teachings.

Sometimes society values don't align with what you teach at home. So, it is imperative to develop a system of values early on that mimic what you believe and what is important to you. When your system is established, it will shine and be evident. Everyone knows where you stand and what your home stands on. When the root system is not grounded and watered in love, it will be shaky and weak. Some foundations have lots of weeds and root weevils. Even though you can't see weevils, these little pests start as larvae eating away at the roots underground. So, when the branches sprout, they are weak and unhealthy. When a system is weak, it is not hard for various ideas and thoughts, that are contrary to your beliefs, to stream in and convince family members that someone else is a better builder or gardener. Not only are they perceived as better gardeners, but as better caretakers of you and your family.

Anything weak that is not firmly planted will sway in the wind and be easily uprooted. Taking extreme care to develop a root system that can withstand the air's harsh elements is how plants and members survive. Remember my grapevine? I did everything to kill it. It would not die.

Now, let's pause. Take a breath. Does that mean that your kids will turn out perfect? No! But, they will have a fighting chance to overcome any obstacle that comes to their path. As we press ahead, you will read about my sons' challenges and mine as a mother, as well as the sustaining lessons that helped us on life's journey.

FOUR ENVIRONMENTAL FACTORS MUST BE IN PLACE #2- SOIL AND RAIN

"Some trust in chariots and some trust in horses, but we trust in the name of the Lord our G-d."

— Psalms 20:7

"I sought the Lord, and He answered me; He delivered me from all my fears."

— Psalms 34:4

"Even to your old age and gray hairs I am He, I am He who sustains you. I have made you, and I will carry you; I will sustain you, and I will rescue you."

— Isaiah 46:4

"Be strong and courageous. Do not be afraid or terrified because of them, for the Lord your G-d goes with you, and He will never leave you nor forsake you."

— Deuteronomy 31:6

The soil is so important in growing plants. It provides an anchor for roots and the nutrients for growth. It filters the rainwater, regulates its delivery to the soil, and prevents flooding. Soil buffers against pollutants, protecting the quality of the groundwater and preserves a record of past conditions. The nutrients in the soil of our foundation had to be rich with the Word of G-d so it could be the filter that sifted my children's thoughts and actions. If they used the Word of G-d as the soil for their belief system, they would have a strong anchor. It was important to me that they relied only on G-d. When pollutants came, with G-d as their anchor, their filtering system would be strong enough to sift out the waste. If my sons searched for a "stone of remembrance," they would have a history in the Word and a foot firmly planted in the soil where they grew up. I didn't want them to get caught up in church mechanics or be distracted by how people acted or what they may or may not say. I only wanted them to know Christ as a personal Savior and Father.

I have always known our G-d as the Almighty, and that He can do anything. If you cry out, He promises to answer. I cannot remember a time without Him. As a young child, I was fascinated by His power. I often wondered why we could not do more or be more. After a while, I realized that we don't know who our Father is. In the last ten years, under new spiritual leadership, Pastor Rob helped me learn more about the Father we serve. He is a Father who sits near us, a Father we can turn to and have a conversation about our day, disappointments, and successes. We don't know who we genuinely serve, who our Father truly is, or the power of that relationship.

Sometimes in relationships, we can use words so loosely that they become rote and lack the depth of understanding and power. But by grace, we can be born again. We can have the chance to follow Jesus and become part of His chosen family. We have an amazing, all-powerful, and loving Father who seeks to care for us at the highest level. As you will pick up from the reading, there is an overriding theme of the love and knowledge of G-d.

I worked very purposefully on this task. I took my children to Sunday school and church every Sunday. Every message was discussed and filtered purposefully for clear understanding or correction, making sure that church service was not a social activity but a place to learn and worship the Father. It was also a place to cultivate a personal relationship with Christ. I understood that if I didn't wrap their minds in the Word of G-d, something else would enter and conquer their minds. I believed that if I instilled these building blocks and cultivated this rich soil, greater chances of survival would surface. I also understood that I still ran the chance of my sons being rebellious, and they were. During their lifetime, I am sure the Lord was not always at the forefront of their actions. But I believed and was confident in the scripture, Proverbs 22:6, "Train up a child in the way he should go, and when he is old, he will not depart from it."

Great care was taken in cultivating this soil with the Word of G-d. I experienced many people telling me about G-d, who He was, the things you had to do to be a believer, the number of times you had to repeat Hallelujah or attend prayer meetings, even how long your skirt had to be, or the denomination that saved lives. To reduce the anxiety of other voices, I tried to set it straight early with my children. We dialogued about faith, what it meant to believe, and who and what you could always trust. Although I wanted them always to trust me, I knew I could fail them even though I would never want to. Even though my heart and mind might have good intentions and desires, I knew that I might fall, lose my senses, or even grow too old to say the right things. My sons needed a firm foundation that would never fail them.

Soil is where roots stretch out and grow. These words are the nutrients that keep the ground prepped to grow. The power and authority granted through the adoption in the family of G-d is what filters out and protects the heart and mind (fruit) that extends from this soil.

FOUR ENVIRONMENTAL FACTORS MUST BE IN PLACE #3 & #4 - SUNLIGHT AND PRUNING

When you prune plants, you cut back the stems, roots, or branches to grow fuller and more beautiful. We do this to plants, and G-d does this for us. I am so glad about it. Pruning done incorrectly can ruin a plant. A plant meant to produce abundant flowers and fruit can be a pitiful sight to see if the gardener is not careful. As we live on Earth, we experience lots of pruning for the life stages we transition through. It is meant to make us wiser, more intelligent, humbler, and compassionate towards everyone we encounter. When the scissors start snipping and reshaping us, it doesn't feel like you can make it through, but I can attest that it is for your good. Our children have to know it is coming. The experiences at home will help them realize that they will make it through.

Sunlight is the gift. The sun reminds us of the life ahead. When you see the brightness of the day or even the hint of light, you know that you have one more day of practice and a day to get it right. The sunlight strengthens your immune system by providing Vitamin D. It reduces illness, infections, and helps you maintain calcium to prevent brittle bones. The sun has the power to give you a better life. It is hard for your plants to live without sunlight. The energy of the sun produces food for the plants to grow, reproduce, and survive. Your home is like a garden. It provides sustaining power through many mechanisms to increase growth, reproduce established values, and implement survival strategies, all from a bit of practice.

HOME IS THE PRACTICE RUN FOR THE REST OF YOUR LIFE...

> *"Do you not know that in a race all the runners run, but only one gets the prize? Run in such a way as to get the prize. (25) Everyone who competes in the games goes into strict training. They do it to get a crown that will not last, but we do it to get a crown that will last forever. (26) Therefore, I do not run like a man running aimlessly; I do not fight like a man beating the air. (27) No, I beat my body and make it my slave so that after I have preached others, I myself will not be disqualified for the prize."*
> — 1 Corinthians 9:24-27

If someone were to ask your name, you wouldn't pause, ponder, or wonder what people call you. That is mastery or perfection. As a principal, I learned that it takes 1,400 practices for a low-performing student to learn anything to the point of being able to repeat it without thinking. It takes an average student about 25-35 practices and a high performing student 10-12 practices to master knowing information. As we think about the number of times it takes to practice anything for perfection, home becomes a great place to get a head start. Family provides a place to be distinguished. Home is where you can practice the art of setting yourself apart from the rest, where you can not only help your loved ones become their best self but also grow more fully into the person G-d intends you to be. Families create high standards at home. It is the place where you practice things that others are not practicing. Home is the practice run because you have coaches around you who can provide feedback on how well you are doing. They help make your skills sharper and better. At home, you are surrounded by people who love you and want to see you succeed. The family can hold the mirror in such a way that you can see yourself front and back and then ask, "Can you see that? Fix this. Straighten up."

Every athlete, musician, or artist practiced their craft to become better and to be excellent—people who are great practice over and over again. I know children look at star athletes, musicians, chefs, beauticians, architects, and writers and don't realize the number of failures or how much practice it took to get to their position in life. They are unaware of the late nights and early mornings, the number of fun things with their friends they had to sacrifice because of the practice they had to do. Home should be like that. Home should be a place not only to sleep, play, eat, and work, but a place to practice the skills to not only survive but to thrive. Home is one of the places where you are surrounded by people who know you, celebrate your triumphs and hand you a tissue in your failures or challenges. It is home where you fall, and family will lift you back up. Home is a privilege and gift!

I do wish I had done more practicing at home with my kids. I wish I practiced more with them to look at themselves and not be afraid of change. I often thought of my parents. They did the best they could with what they knew. We learn from our parents, so we have an opportunity to do so much more. We have a chance to maximize everything that is in our immediate surroundings and send our children soaring on the planet.

Home is the practice run for the rest of our children's life. Every step, lesson, and experience are valued and can be used for their success or demise. These lessons are intended to set you apart, make you look different, and grab others' attention. Training and practicing change your level of accomplishment and automatically move you to another level of existence.

Practice and perfect practice allow you to improve your skills and be the best at what you do. How you act sets you apart! For example, manners are an effortless way to have someone take a second look. Simple words like "thank you", "please", and "you are welcome" create an atmosphere or culture that allows people to forget about themselves and look at the person who is speaking. We can no longer believe our kids will catch the information in the air, that it will come, or that it is unnecessary to practice little skills to make them better.

I have not spent a lot of time talking about the importance of education, but education is essential for taking care of yourself. Learn something that will render you a livable wage that is non-negotiable. But, in addition to an excellent education, learn some skills and lessons to seal the deal so the job interviewer will say, "I want you!"

We cannot afford to let our children's minds be developed outside of the home or trust that someone else will do a better job, unless we believe it to be so. The time and effort you invest in your child will pay off in the end. There is no escape from challenges, but there is the opportunity to be prepared to handle them.

WHERE DO WE START?

For most of my life, I have not felt super smart. Many times I felt inadequate and unsure of myself. I had no silver spoon or money to start my life or unique gifts to get me started on my journey. My Sunday school teacher taught us about G-d, and I believed her when she said, "He is the G-d Almighty." I learned many lessons by trial and error. I have won and lost, but the only constant in my life was my trust and belief in G-d and my need to depend on Him.

Over the years, I built a personal relationship with G-d, not church, religion, or activities, but G-d. I found my relationship with Him to be reliable, unmovable, and unbreakable. He never lets my feelings or emotions hamper how He provided for me or loved me. His love has carried me through significant challenges with personal relationships, jobs, and children. I have cried—no—I have sobbed and been broken, but the emotional and financial impact of every circumstance has been for my good.

Life is a school. You have many classes with many lessons. Some courses are challenging, while others are easy. Some classes have many studies and standards of learning while others are quick and easy, but the degree of difficulty does not matter. You must pass the final exam.

Interestingly, the lessons of life start simple and serve as the foundation for the next course. Sometimes you get a good teacher and sometimes not. In the class, unlearned lessons are continuously repeated. Sometimes you stay after class to receive additional help to increase your skills to do better. When you don't practice the skills necessary to pass the lesson at age 10, you will find yourself trying to pass the same study at age 25. You have to forget all the wrong stuff you practiced and understood and retain the suitable material to succeed.

Home is the place to practice with people. Many life lessons require you to demonstrate your ability to think critically about what people say and do, how to interact with people at work and school, and contribute to people's well-being in your community. Working with people is the biggest and most critical lesson to learn in life, and it is not in the school curriculum. There is no course called "The skills of working with people," maybe with the exception of Kindergarten. Our world consists of people like me, you, our neighbors, and others. For our loved ones to conquer the world, they must learn the lessons of being with people. Practice! Consider what should be in your training packet and the skills you know you should practice like tasks you don't do well, and ones you would love to master.

I have included practical and spiritual life lessons, as well as soft skills for your everyday life. First, read to the end of the book, then concentrate on some skills and lessons to prioritize your first month. Work on them. When you have learned one lesson, move to another. If you knew these lessons early in life, share them with your neighbors. Involve your relatives and the entire neighborhood in preparation for a more excellent quality of life.

Just recently, my niece Michelle showed me the importance of practicing these lessons. Michelle is an excellent example of always wanting to do better. We call each other, not for any particular reason other than to check in, but it always ends in a lesson. Recently, she was concerned about not having enough money to buy ornaments for Christmas. Once, she saw ornaments on my tree and said she could not afford them. They looked too expensive. She was right, but I didn't pay a high price. I am the queen of bargain shopping. Nothing in my closet or house is full price. If it doesn't say 75% off, I probably don't own it. I told her that I buy ornaments at the end of the season for the following year. Instead of worrying about what she didn't have, I encouraged her to start her traditions.

Her daughter Maia loves to draw. They could make personalized ornaments—an extraordinary way to promote her love for art by seeing her artwork on the tree. Daily, Maia could marvel at her handiwork. She could engage in conversations with her friends at school about their tradition of making handmade ornaments and saving them year after year. We thought about the many lessons that could come from making ornaments: budgeting, learning about each other, creating traditions, the value of time, work, and the gift of being creative.

Your only failure is in not doing. People talk. Successful people do. And believe me, you would be surprised by the number of people who start and don't finish. I am no different. Since 2017 I have tried to write this book. I have talked about it and dreamed about it. My son Corey would tell me about the people who finished their books. He would say things like, "Just start! Just do something."

He would send me screenshots of individuals at his conferences with their books and ask, "Can't you do this?"

I started writing on scratch paper, big post-it paper, little note stickers, but no book. This year was different. Contained in the house, I just believed that if I did not get it done this year, my window of opportunity would pass me. Just think, if I didn't start, there would be no need for the Lord to send me an angel to hear and read my words, to edit and help me complete my goal. The Lord always wants the best for us. He will help you when you are ready to be supported.

I reflected on how much I could have done and how much more I could have practiced these lessons and skills. Since I have learned just a few things, my hope lies in you to use these lessons to help your family be more than you could ever imagine possible.

But You.

Every day I look back on my life
Thoughts come and go
Lessons misinterpreted
Teachable moments gone and by
I thought I needed to be perfect for you
But perfection wasn't ever asked of me
I thought expectations were too high
But I wasn't thinking high enough
I believed in other Gods
Though you were only teaching one
Oh, the struggles we've seen
The mountains we've climbed
The deserts we've slowly crossed
Misconceived
Misconstrued
Falling backwards and forwards
But You.
You are always the constant
Never giving up on me
Even when I gave up on myself

You are my strength
You are my heart
You are my light
Even when I couldn't see
All I hear in my heart
And in my mind is blessed
For that I am eternally grateful
But You.
Even through it all
The pain
The anguish
The sleepless nights
And the letting go
The tears
The fear
The unknown
You still looked up to the sky
With arms wide open
Giving me over to the Lord
A loving sacrifice made so dear
Oh that letting go
The greatest gift of all
But You.

LINDA GIBSON FLETCHER, PhD

Helped me find me again
But You.
Helped me have a second chance
Truly humbling beyond doubt
So, I look back on those days
Thinking of the things I missed
The lessons I got wrong
And the signs I couldn't see
With the wisdom I have now
And the gratitude in my heart
I fall to my knees
Because You
You taught me faith
That lasts forever
You taught me love
With all my heart
And most importantly
You taught me about God

By Alan Tyson
2020

Part I

God First

"The earth is the Lord's and everything in it, the world, and all who live in it; for He founded it upon the seas and established it upon the waters."

— PSALMS 24:1-2

"Jesus answered, "Everyone who drinks this water will be thirsty, but whoever drinks the water I give him will never thirst. Indeed, the water I give him will become in him a spring of water welling up to eternal life."

— JOHN 4:13-14

"Those who know your name will trust in you, for you, Lord, have never forsaken those who seek you."

— PSALMS 9:10

"Teach them to your children, talking about them when you sit at home and when you walk along the road, when you lie down and when you get up."

— DEUTERONOMY 11:19

1

Know G-d as the Almighty

*T*HE BIBLE IS THE LIVING, precious Word of G-d. It is the story of G-d Himself. Every lesson we need in life is in the Bible on how to live on Earth and enjoy the abundance of the physical and spiritual life intended by G-d Almighty. It has living examples and spiritual insight on how to become loving, prosperous, and how you can successfully live with others. Being adopted into His Family gives us rights, power, and authority to have Him as a Father and to be heir to everything He owns. If you don't know Him, much of what I say may not make much sense to you. But I employ you to keep reading, and maybe the verses introduced at the beginning of every section will resonate inside, and you may find yourself asking, "G-d, who are you?" By the time you finish, you will know Him, and it will all make more sense.

"For G-d so loved the world, that He gave His one and only Son, whoever believes in Him shall not perish but have eternal life."

— John 3:16

"Even to your old age and gray hairs I am He, I am He who will sustain you. I have made you, and I will carry you; I will sustain you, and I will rescue you."

— Isaiah 46:4

"I sought the Lord, and He answered me; He delivered me from all my fears."

— Psalms 34:4

"And my G-d shall supply all your needs according to His riches in glory in Christ Jesus."

— Philippians 4:19

Throughout my children's life (birth-college) we would ride home from Sunday church service and discuss the lesson or sermon. If I found one eye closing during service, I'd nudge them and raise my eyebrow to indicate that they needed to stay awake in church. There were no coloring books, no talking, no playing or sleeping. Bibles and ears were open. Following the service, there was always a teachable moment. Man could make an error, but not the Word of G-d. If a response or action contradicted the Word of G-d, I quickly corrected it in the car before we made it home to the dinner table. Questionable sermons heard in church or other places weren't left for the boys to ponder or figure out independently.

There was more than just showing up on Sundays and Wednesdays. I believed in the power of G-d and His Word. Since I was a little girl, I always wanted to experience the miracle-working power of the Lord. Attending many churches and listening to the Word of G-d, I knew that there was something more. Something was missing. It was hard to quantify it or put what I learned into words, but I wanted my boys to find it early.

As I experienced much in life, it taught me the value of the price of our life. Our Father in heaven gave His only Son so that we could be in a relationship with Him. He loved us that much. Our Father did more for my family and me than anyone can or will ever do. I hoped my sons would know Him as a passionate and loving Father who sought only their best. I wanted them to see how He never slept. He walked the Earth, moving things and people around to ensure that what He planned for each of us was completed. That was and is an amazing love! We never have to feel powerless or hopeless because we have G-d as a Father.

Since we know who we belong to, we don't have to act powerless and helpless. I want you to know I love saying that our Father is the Almighty and Jesus is our brother. Do you know what that means? My Father, your Father, desires what is right and perfect for you! He has a design for you! Your plan is not my design. I can never take anything from you. It can't be stolen, manipulated, or destroyed because it is not for the taking. What's for me and for you can never be stolen. Many people will try, but they can't. When you know that nothing can be taken from you, you are free to help people without fear. You can share your talent and resources, and your well will not run dry.

The Father is available and willing to keep your vessel filled to the brim and running over. If you believe and trust in Him, His love is available. Our Father has everything we need. You will try to find that thing to make you happy, complete you, and help you be strong, but it will never be enough. If you are not locked into a real power source, that superpower, then you will find power in other places, like gangs, drugs, alcohol, sex, work, and even unhealthy relationships.

It is essential to teach kids about G-d's power source early so their reliance is appropriate. You will wonder and try to figure out where you belong. Ultimately, that search may destroy you. I have seen it with my sons. They forgot that G-d was everything they needed. The only saving grace is that they knew how to call out. When they called out, our Father, our G-d, heard them and rescued them. That didn't alleviate any consequences, but when saved from their circumstance, they knew it was only the Lord because the outcome could have been unimaginably worse. They remembered what they learned and practiced all those years. They recognized that being with G-d was better than being without Him.

If you have not considered asking Jesus into your life (John 3:16), then you have an opportunity. If you are reading this, your time is not up. I encourage you to call upon Him. He will answer. He desires to be your Father.

How will you teach this lesson?

This lesson is about knowing G-d. I encourage you to get a Bible. Read the Bible or listen to the Bible on tape and follow along in your Bible. Open up the book to St. John and start reading with the entire family. If you earnestly seek G-d, He will be found. He promises. Reading the Bible is not about making you feel good. It is about getting to know the ways of your new-found Family of G-d. The Bible has all the answers to life. But the answers are hidden deep in the Word to be uncovered by the people of G-d. They are treasures for anyone who wants to know Him.

Consider relationships you have been in. They took time to develop. Our Father is the same way. If you start early teaching this lesson, your family will practice reading the Bible and using the lessons and teachings to guide their personal lives. You will find the deep treasures of their life. But you have to put in the work to understand the Father's dreams and hopes for you. Earnestly pray to G-d to know Him as your Lord, Savior, and Father.

Finally, find a church home where the activities are not the focal point and the Word of G-d is at the center. Find a place where you will grow in His Word and ways. Finally, find a place where you practice G-d's love, and you can see people's lives changing because of the power of the Almighty G-d.

How will you see the lesson in practice?

- Your children will ask to read more about G-d.
- They will ask you to take them to a church or hear a lesson on TV where they are teaching the Word of G-d.
- They will ask you about your beliefs and then question some of your behaviors.
- They may ask about what is right and wrong.
- Your family will change to be more loving and giving.

⟶ **Notes from My Sons** ⟵

I can do all things through Christ that strengthens me. I took this lesson to heart. I truly believed that God had my back and that there were no limitations to my success. I still believe in this life lesson to this day. What is interesting about this life lesson was the reality of my humanity. I mean, humans, we are so often limited to what we can create in our specific and personal worlds. Although our worldly success should be attributed to our Heavenly Father, we often self-gratify when we achieve some success level. In this lesson, I learned that nothing good happens for a believer without God's hands and work in it.

— Corey

If I have not learned anything else in my life, I knew who and what God is. I learned to believe in a higher power. If I have not learned anything else in my life, I have always known to have faith. I have learned to look to the Holy Bible for answers, and I have grown to understand that you cannot go on in life without Him. I believe I started as an infant sitting at the dinner table for a very long time. It seemed as though it was all day long because I couldn't recite or tell what the church lesson was about. I remember going to church functions and trying not to fall asleep, then becoming an adult, going to church with my friends, and then being an adult, making sure God is in all aspects of my life. It's all because of you. You have etched God into my brain, mind, heart, hands, feet, and every living fiber of my being. God is the way. God is the key. God is everything. I thank you for that lesson.

— Alan

Be comfortable with discomfort because God is still forming you into who He is designing you to become.

— Renny, Jr.

Keep God first no matter how great you do and how low you get; He will always be there for you.

— Renny, Jr.

Love your passions because it comes from God. Never waver from what God has planned for you because God will reroute you back to what He prepared you to do. It just depends on how long you want it to take, to see what great things He has in store.

—Renny, Jr.

"Those who know your name will trust in you, for you, Lord, have never forsaken those who seek you."

— PSALM 9:10

"Call to Me, and I will answer you, and show you great and might things which you do not know."

— JEREMIAH 33:3

"Ask, and it will be given to you, see, and you will find; know, and it will be opened to you."

— MATTHEW 7:7

"Is anything too hard for the Lord?"

— GENESIS 18:14

"Be anxious for nothing, but in everything by prayer and supplication, with thanksgiving, let your requests be made known to G-d.

— PHILIPPIANS 4:6

2

Prayer

ARLY IN MY EDUCATIONAL CAREER, I spent months on the road consulting around the country. Alan called me. He was in distress, and I wasn't near to comfort or console him. I knew his heart hurt, but I could only talk with him over the phone. At that moment, I reminded him what I learned. I would not always be near to comfort him, but I knew the Lord would. I reminded him to pour his heart out to the Lord, and He would hear him.

It is essential to know and believe G-d as the Father and as a person in which you develop a personal relationship. We have a direct link through faith in Jesus and the opportunity to have an intimate relationship. He is someone you can get up with in the morning, talk with in the afternoon, get to know in the evening moment, and allow Him to tell you what He knows of you.

Prayer provides a line to open up and share our deepest and

darkest secrets that He will not reveal to others. He will hear us and love us despite our failures, frailties, and sins. Our amazing Father has nothing but love for us. Teaching your child to cry out to the Lord for all things helps them see the power of their relationship and the power of the G-d they serve.

Renny, Jr., in the simplest ways, cried out to the Lord. *"Lord, please let there be a bowling alley open so we can have a family day."* Or *"Lord, please let my mommy have this baby tonight."*

Every single time he prayed an earnest prayer, G-d answered, right before our eyes. I don't mean to teach them about a "candy store," but a person who can be a friend, an all-knowing and powerful person you grow to love. Without studying the Word of G-d, it is hard to develop a relationship. The Word of G-d provides everything you need to live a successful life.

Alan recently shared with me that, "Everything I need to know is in the Bible. I should have read more."

We all look back and say we should have read more. But it is not too late. If you are reading this, you still have time to do more and be more.

Building this foundation is not done in a day. It is built brick by brick. Having daily conversations, not just about your wants and dreams, but who you are, what you feel, what you think, where you are going, and where you want to be, builds a fantastic relationship not with just G-d the Lord Almighty, but with G-d your Father. Each day you can discuss everything with G-d. My hope was for my children, grandchildren, and their grandchildren to learn and know to talk to G-d.

I did not know G-d as my Father until I was well over 50. I

knew G-d almighty, but not G-d the Father. I think it is because I did not have an example of that kind of relationship with my dad.

I never experienced this "call on my dad, and he will come running." My dad was a nice man, and I knew he loved me and admired me as his daughter and as a woman. He always told me how proud he was of me, but I never felt like I could go to him to help me or that he would be there if I needed something. Early on as a child, my dad promised me a dress for 6th grade graduation, and the time came for him to give it to me. He didn't. This experience caused me to be reluctant about asking him for anything. I was afraid of being disappointed. Knowing G-d as a Father never really dawned on me as significant. But it is!

Having a Father illuminates the vision of having this conversation about your day easier. Prayer allows for intimacy. You can't be vulnerable, honest, and open to comments or consequences without putting time in with a person or your Lord. G-d already knows you, but when you spend time in prayer and the Word of G-d, you get the opportunity to learn about Him. Knowing Him grants you this one immense privilege of being confident in who He is and how much He loves you.

Intimacy requires work and practice. Pastor Rob teaches us to set a time to check in with the Lord before our day starts, mid-day (like 3:00), and before we fall asleep at night. Tell Him what you have been through and where you are going. Catch Him up. I know some siblings who check-in 3 and 4 times a day with each other. Can you imagine the kind of intimacy they have developed being intertwined with one another so often?

A love relationship is a two-way experience. I talk, but I also listen. It flows back and forth. The Lord has a lot to say, but when He speaks, it is crucial. He is too great for chit-chat. Remember, in the Old Testament? People feared the Lord talking. Why? Lives changed. He spoke, and the world could stop. He spoke, and it rained 40 days and 40 nights. He spoke, and the sea divided. Everything He says and does is with great purpose. It is for your good and His glory.

He cares about everything that concerns you. He may not give an opinion on the color of your hair, but if it matters to you, it matters to Him. One time, I was saving for an expensive purse. I wanted it very badly. A friend told me I would not be able to own that purse for the money I had put aside. But I am here to say the Lord answered my prayer, even about a handbag. I got that purse for the amount that I saved.

I remember I just finished college, and Renny, Jr. had turned 2 years old. It was time to get to work. I was a teacher, but they were not hiring teachers at the time. I worked as a substitute teacher, but I needed full-time employment. I started looking at all kinds of places for all types of jobs. I only had one perfect navy blue suit for interviews. There was no time for me to waste. I couldn't afford to get my suit cleaned over and over again. I shared this with the Lord and explained why I couldn't hop from interview to interview. Plus, it was July and August. There was no air in school buildings, no air walking from the car to the establishments. I sweated heavily. I had one good chance with my only blue suit to have a good interview. But something happened after one particular interview. When I arrived, there were 15 people in the room with me. A man came in and told us this job was the dream of a lifetime and that we could make a lot of money selling something. I didn't even hear the last words he spoke. I ruined my only interview suit with sweat. Plus, it was not only hot, but I had to pay for a babysitter and use gas on a limited budget.

I said, "Lord, I can't do door to door. You have to bring me an opportunity. I need it today."

What do you think happened? Before Labor Day, I had a job. I subbed in a building, and the principal remembered me. She told me about a teaching job at a Catholic school. The rest was history. I cried out, and I was serious. So much was on the line. I had a limited amount of money and only a few changes of clothes. I needed a job with a steady income and benefits, so I asked the Lord, and He answered in a couple of weeks. There was not one second that I doubted the Lord would answer my prayer. I knew it would happen, but I just didn't know how. Prayer is the only way to know the Father. I wanted this for my children because I knew that they could not fail if they got this right, no matter what happened in their life.

When I took Renny Jr. to preschool, I had to fill out a questionnaire. One of the questions asked what was most important to me. I said, "Him knowing G-d." There is one guarantee in life. Challenges will come because life is not without them, but if our children practice and pray, praying could become a way of life. Our children could overcome, champion through, and be better because of the experience. It has held for all of my children. They had problems, some I could see coming and others I couldn't, but they called out to the Lord with each situation and circumstance, and He answered. They didn't escape the consequences of their behavior, but the results never took them out of the game of life, even though it could have.

Prayer is me talking to G-d about this journey as a mother, wife, and friend. When I don't think I am enough for my husband, when I think he needs more from me and I don't know how to give it, and when my kids need advice and I want to present it in a way that won't crush their spirit, I pray for a way to deliver the information. I pray for a way to listen so I can hear even what they are not saying. Even at work, I asked the Lord to show me things that I could not see with my eyes. Uncover all things that would get in the way of me leading and being a better leader.

Prayer is critical to your humbleness. It is essential to know you're vulnerable to the world, but you have a power greater than yourself to help overcome this world. G-d lives in you to do all things. Not some things. *All* things. Knowing who you belong to gives you rights and entitlement. The only way to not have is to not fully understand the power and ability of the One you serve. If you knew that your earthly dad could give you anything, do anything, be anywhere for you, wouldn't you call on him? Remember how I told you about my dad? I didn't call on him because I didn't believe he could help me. Our Heavenly Father can do anything.

A Side Note

Based on my experience, it is essential, if you can, to help kids know they can rely on you. Show them, not by buying things, but by being there to hear them, to hold them, to listen to them, not always giving a teachable moment, but letting them know you care. Take time to show them, in the Word of G-d, how the

Father cared for his friends and the people He loved. Pray with them and write down their prayers and concerns. Timestamp them in a notebook or your Bible. Let them hear you cry out. Let them listen to you pray and let them watch G-d work in your life so they will know that He is real.

How do you do teach this lesson?

Pray in front of your kids. Pray about them and about you leading them. I invite you to discuss the power of prayer openly. Don't use a script or formal words but have a conversation. Practice when you wake up, at lunch, and at dinner. Pray when something goes wrong or right and when you need something. When a problem occurs that is not a life-or-death situation, ask your child to pray so they can see what the Lord says. Begin praying as well. Pray when things go well.

Recently, Alan asked me, "Mom, are you happy about finishing your *Get Smart* book?"

I said, "Well, I guess."

He said, "You guess?! You better fall on your knees and thank G-d! Mom, what you accomplished is huge! Don't wait for something bigger. Stop and thank G-d, now!"

I guess I got a lesson.

How will you see the lesson in practice?

- Children will discuss their conversations with the Lord. You will hear their prayers as they pray over breakfast, lunch, and dinner. They will respond very similarly to how Alan told me! "Mom, you better pray."

❧ **Notes from My Sons** ❧

Prayer creates a personal relationship between you and God. To grow, you must establish your relationship.

— Renny, Jr.

The most valuable thing about prayer that you taught me was that God listens and gives you exactly what you want (maybe not HOW you want it but exactly how you need it). We must cry out our trials and tribulations and fall to our knees with celebrations and gratitude for all God does for us. We do this through prayer.

—Alan

What I learned from you mom is to pray about everything. Ask God to make my path clear and give me an understanding of my current life's circumstances. Take time to reflect and think.

— Corey

"He replied, because you have so little faith. I tell you the truth, if you have faith as small as a mustard seed, you can say to this mountain, 'Move from here to there,' and it will move. Nothing would be impossible for you."

— MATTHEW 17:20

"I will say of the Lord, "He is my refuge and my fortress, my God, in whom I trust."

— PSALM 91:2

"Some trust in chariots and some in horses, but we trust in the name of the Lord our G-d."

— PSALMS 20:7

"And my G-d shall supply all your needs according to His riches in glory in Christ Jesus."

— PHILIPPIANS 4:19

3

Faith

WHAT IS FAITH?

*H*EBREWS 11:1 READS, "NOW FAITH is confidence in what we hope for and assurance about we do not see." I love this verse. We have confidence solely in our G-d. Not in ourselves, not anything others say, but in G-d Himself.

Faith is assurance in what we do not see. Think about that statement. Let that resonate in your thinking. Today we live in environments where trust is put in your skills, education, who you know, who someone else knows, and even what or who you can buy for your success. While I believe in increasing and perfecting your skills and getting the highest form of education and experiences, there is a factor that outweighs them all, and that is faith in G-d. I have been in several situations where only G-d could have orchestrated it.

One Spring day, I was in Texas on a research assignment, and the superintendent from Mississippi called to my mentor's school building to ask if anyone knew how to contact me.

I was standing next to the person who answered the call. My kids have witnessed that type of faith in action in my life and theirs.

One time I quit a job because it didn't seem right. My daughter Ugochi begged me not to leave until I found another job. I refused and submitted my resignation. An hour later, someone called to offer me a job. Every aspect of my life has happened in that manner. I wanted to change positions at another job, and the person in charge said, "Absolutely not!" She continued to tell me that I had not paid my dues and others had been in the company longer. But G-d. By the end of the year, she was offering me the promotion.

My faith is not in me but G-d. I have confidence in Him, not me. My kids remind me all the time that it is not me; it is G-d. Never put your trust in the things you can see. What you see is deceptive. It is not the reality of the world in which you live. Never let that dictate your end.

When Renny Jr. and Corey played sports, I was the mom yelling from the stands that the game was not over and telling them not to give up! In the twinkling of an eye, anything could happen because you cannot judge or quantify the elements that move heaven and earth. I would share with all the boys that our G-d has to move many things around to make sure He provides the best for us. Time is not relevant to the G-d of all humanity. He is the only person who knows what the end will look like, so have faith and stay connected.

In our world, you are asked to have faith in your employer, spouse, parents, and friends, but none of those individuals can rescue you from unforeseen circumstances. None of them know what the end will look like, what lies ahead, what hole is covered, who is getting ready to deceive, or who isn't your friend. They don't know, and because they don't know, you have to practice putting your faith in the only one who does know.

I clown with Alan a lot because I will tell him something, and 98% of the time he will not believe me even though it is true. I look at him and giggle because I have experience with people. I watch behavior all the time. I observe what people do and don't do. I keep the information with me. When I need to decide what to do, I examine my database, and I tell Alan what will happen next. I have done that all of my life. We serve a G-d that takes my little interest in people to the tenth degree. He blows it out of the ballpark.

Our G-d is making a road map. "For I know the plans I have for you, plans to give you hope and a future" (Jeremiah 29:11). Our God is working out everything to bring you "hope and a future." He is doing this not just for me but for you. He has a specific plan for your life, which looks different than the plan for my life. All of my children are different. Each child needs food, water, shelter, and clothes. While they need all of the same basics to live, the things they like, their passions, their interests, and what drives them are different. As a parent, I related to them based on their various desires, how they responded and reacted to directions and discipline, and how quickly they learned lessons. Our G-d operates similarly, except He knows your precise needs, how you will respond, and the number of practices required so that you enjoy the fullness of His "hope and future" for you.

I was divorced. But I never lost hope that I would find true love. I believed that G-d would send me the one to be with me all the days of my life. I've divorced three times. I hate writing that, but it is true. Each experience helped me understand the person that should be with me. Pastor Rob would lessen my pain by telling me to marry until I got it right. I believe he was joking, but he knew I wanted true love. So I trusted that G-d would make it happen. I met my future husband Roosevelt, Jr. while ordering some shirts for my students, but it wasn't until three years later when I realized he was the one.

One day I needed some t-shirts to give to my weekly Thursday night dinner friends, the Amazing Kroger Crew (AKC). Every Thursday, we dined at Kroger. It was the best! They served a 3-course meal and three flights of wine ranging from $10-$25.00. We always met, giggled, ate the chef's favorite prepared meals, and selected wine for each course for the evening. I wanted to make shirts for this group. I started these shirts on my own but, I didn't have the skills to finish the job. I was desperate. I needed to get my design on these shirts. My oldest son Renny, Jr., said he would call the person he worked with to see if he could get me in. He did!

When I met him, there was something special about him. We made each other laugh. He talked about my work and assured me he could do a better job and have it on the day I needed it. The moment I left his office, I asked my son if he was married. Who was he? Did he know anything about his personal life? What did he know? My son reluctantly told me nothing. He shut me down fast, but there's something ironic about how G-d moves.

The Lord had to get me to Kroger, create friendships, and put in my heart to do something for them. Then the Lord caused my project to fail, created an opening in Roosevelt's schedule, and made sure he was free and not dating. When I returned to pick up my shirts, looking all sassy, I could share with him, "If you ever want to hang out, my phone number is on the invoice."

What did he do? After my event, he called. The rest was history. As of 2020, we have been married for three years.

Do you see how many people, places, and things G-d moved for my one prayer to be answered? You have to be confident and sure of who you trust. Plus, you cannot add in a little of this or little of that and get faith. You have to be confident in who you serve. If He said it, believe it. I don't mean old wise tales or some made up thing. I mean, if G-d said it, He can do more than you could ever think or imagine. If G-d says have faith the size of a mustard seed and you can move a mountain, believe it. If G-d says He is the creator of ALL things and that He is first and the last, believe Him. If He says He's working all things out for your good and His glory, believe it.

"Being confident of this, that He who began a good work in you will carry it on to completion until the day of Jesus Christ." (Philippians 1:6)

How do you teach this lesson?

If they have a desire or a need, send them to G-d. Try not to always be the answer. Tell them to ask G-d first before they ask you. If you need to know how to help, the Lord will guide you. G-d can give you what you need to help every child.

How will you see it in practice?

- They will report on what happened. Your children will explain how the Lord delivered them, heard their prayers, and answered them. They will share how they believed He could help them and how He did.

❧ Notes from My Sons ☙

As far as I can remember, and even today, she has always told me
to "Live by faith. Never by sight!"

— Renny, Jr.

At times in your life, when things don't go your way, you start
to waver. I remember talking to mom, and she would say, "Why
do you worry so much if you say you have faith?" Immediately,
I would snap out of my funk and say, "She's right." and thank
God for my life.

— Renny, Jr.

Part II

Soft Skills

"...equip you with everything good for doing his will, and may he work in us what is pleasing to him, through Jesus Christ, to whom be glory for ever and ever. Amen."

— Hebrews 13:21

"Those who know your name will trust in you, for you, Lord, have never forsaken those who seek you."

— PSALM 9:10

"Call to Me, and I will answer you, and show you great and might things which you do not know."

— JEREMIAH 33:3

"Ask, and it will be given to you, see, and you will find; know, and it will be opened to you."

— MATTHEW 7:7

"Is anything too hard for the Lord?"

— GENESIS 18:14

"Be anxious for nothing, but in everything by prayer and supplication, with thanksgiving, let your requests be made known to G-d.

— PHILIPPIANS 4:6

1

Goal Setting/ Purpose

EVERY SEPTEMBER, WHEN MY BOYS were school aged, we sat at the kitchen table and carved out a chore list and educational, personal, and spiritual goals. As a teacher, the beginning of my year was not January but September. The boys started back to school, so it was a new beginning. Honestly, I have no idea why I started this practice other than wanting them to get in the habit of making a plan, and more importantly, discussing who they were and could become.

I read many self-help books throughout my life. In the books that I read, the authors operated with a plan. Rarely did they float through life. They planned their lives with purpose. If they saw something missing in their community or their business, they created a plan to fill the hole. If their plan didn't work, they were not afraid to redefine or edit their original method to do something different. The authors of these books were fearless in their attempts to be successful. So, I believed developing these skills early on would create a firm foundation for my children's success.

Studying African American history, I felt the oppression of our race. I wanted to minimize and dispel the myth of others' possible views by preparing them to articulate and be transparent in conversations about where they were going and who they wanted to be. It would help others take notice and say they are not like others.

The common thread that runs through everything we do at home and school is the practice run for the rest of their life. These conversations with my sons showed their strengths and weaknesses and improved upon them while setting goals to progress and keep moving. We did not determine goals in isolation but as a family, so my flaws were also up for discussion. My goals were on the table, and we all came to a common understanding of how we would be, act, care, and hold our family accountable.

The conversation with them was an opportunity for me to make goals on how I interacted with them and the things I needed to improve upon as a mother. Additionally, I wanted my boys comfortable with honest evaluation. I wanted them to welcome the experience and begin honestly reflecting on how to be better. The goals they came up with were their own. The only ones they could not negotiate were their chores. They may have been able to negotiate the length of time or when their chores happened, but not the specific jobs. We posted our goals on the refrigerator as a reminder of what we agreed to follow. We allowed everyone at the table to speak honestly.

The lesson is to practice goal-setting, reflecting over your week, month, and year. Be purposeful about reflecting on how you practice these life skills in all aspects of your life, especially personally and professionally. (A student's job is to go to school, participate in sports, do chores, and participate in extra-curricular activities, etc.).

Finally, discuss how you are as a family and how you can do better. The word of G-d gives guides on how to live. Set aside time to discuss it. I encourage you to Facetime family members or pick up the phone and talk. Check-in.

How do you teach this lesson?

Consider goal setting and review an annual event. Make it memorable and encourage the kids to set the agenda, time, date, and order of speakers. Assign who will be the recorder, timekeeper, and more. Time to meet with each other costs nothing. Have some paper and pencil, even snacks and drinks. Make announcements about the upcoming event. Pump it up! Remember some categories:

- How are the chores going? Are any changes, praises, improvements needed?
- Schedule areas (school/work/home) of your life you would you like to improve upon. How? (Accountability)
  - How is your spiritual life? (Praying, tithing, going to church)
  - What are things you have become good at doing?
  - What do you want to become?

How will know you see it in practice?

- Review the meeting notes: Check-in in two weeks, monthly, quarterly

ᨳᨳ Notes from My Sons ᨳᨳ

It's so interesting to be 35 now and understand all those tutoring sessions with Ms. Angela Mosely back in elementary school. We had to be the smartest little guys in the world to make it in our house. Both mom and dad did not play with educational success. It shaped me and molded me into believing that education was vital. I now see why! So many young people speak broken English, cannot write or even read. They don't understand how to add or subtract. The little sessions set us up with a foundation for the rest of our lives. If I had skipped those tutoring sessions, I would be in a different place in life. Thanks, Aunt/Ms. Angela.

— Corey

2

Finances/Save

*N*OT TOO LONG AGO, MY son Alan said to me, "I wish you would have given me a credit card and taught me how to manage it."

Corey even said, "Mom, why didn't you teach us about 401K, stocks, and investments?"

If I told them about the danger of losing control and putting themselves in debt at an early stage, it would cause them to be careful and more explorative with their money. Based on the conversation with Alan and Corey, I think finances is an essential lesson. When my boys graduated college, I gave them self-help books on financial independence as Christmas gifts or found a book for a memorable event to share. I struggled with credit cards in my late 20's and early 30's, and I was out of control. I knew the value of money, but it did not stop me from spending. I wanted my sons to see the value of money as soon as possible.

All of my children had savings accounts, but they did not receive an allowance, nor were they given money to manage. Renny Jr. had a paper route from middle school until he finished high school. Corey and Alan worked as soon as they could get hired. No one managed that money or told them how to spend it, except tithing, which was a requirement. That was not a good practice. We should have had a lesson on money: things to do and not do, how to save, and how to make your money work for you. I knew the only thing to teach was the danger of credit cards: don't get into debt by acquiring credit cards you cannot pay. Extreme debt prevents one from speaking out for what is right and what is needed.

If they didn't have credit obligations, they would be able to take care of themselves and their community.

We lived in Columbus's inner city because we wanted and were insistent on our children knowing the responsibility of caring for their community. The only way to understand our community was to live in it.

My sons received these tools to guide their thinking. Whether they read it or not, they had the information. I wish I knew more and that I had done a better job of educating them about finances.

Renny, Jr. came home from college, and the rule was that he could stay at home, work, and save. He was allowed to practice the financial lesson on saving at home to live debt-free on his own in the next couple of years. About the 10th month, our check-in time was to see how the lesson on savings was going with Renny, Jr., my oldest son. This process was "trial and error" for his siblings.

I knew his gross salary.

I asked, "How much had you saved out of the $35,000.00?" He said, "$200.00."

I fell over in shock. I told Renny, Jr. to get a realtor or he would not see his hard-earned money I wouldn't allow him to get an apartment; it had to be a house. He still owns his home 18 years later.

Three financial principles are critical for life: giving (tithing), saving, and living. Try diligently to give first, then save, and then live. It is always good to remember who provides our resources. Remembering who created Heaven and the Earth helps you give back a portion of the gift freely given to you. If you get good at practicing the three principles of finances, you will never be without money.

You may have lean years, but you will have food and shelter. You may not spend a lot or have a lot saved, but you will have some money or access to it. When your child acquires $100.00 in their savings, open a Roth IRA as soon as possible. It serves as an interest-saving account they can use down the road. If you learn these principles or skills, you can never be without the resources to live.

If you are not an expert on making your money work, sign up for everyone in your family to take a lesson at the bank on money management. Some banks offer these classes to their clients. Financial struggles and hard times may appear but make no mistake. The Lord always shows up. I taught giving and living. I did not teach a lot on saving, but it is critical. The more you practice, the better you can save, especially if you do it early in life and consistently practice it.

How do you teach this lesson?

If you have a financial plan, discuss it. My girlfriend Darcel openly speaks to her daughter about their finances. She might say, "We cannot afford it this week, but maybe next week when I get paid." Or "You can make a choice, but you cannot have both."

Inquire about a Roth IRA. Open a college savings account, especially when your children are little. Using $50.00 to open a college savings and adding $10.00 or $25.00 a month over ten years is a lot of money for you to fund college, tech school, etc. Realistically, you can spend $25.00 at McDonald's or Starbucks weekly. This investment is once a month.

When kids earn or receive money, provide them with a notebook. The general rule is tithe or give in a charity jar (10%) and save 20% (increase if they are not responsible for bills or school-related items/rentals) and the rest of the money is for daily living cost and other items they want to purchase. Even if you have a little, give. It is important.

How will you see it in practice?

- Kids and adults will get out their notebooks and record giving, savings, and spending.
- Review your bank and investment statements.
- Count money in the piggy bank and home.

~&~ Notes from My Sons ~&~

Don't spend everything in one place. Designate a time to spend a specific amount of money.

— Corey

"Never get a credit card" is the biggest thing I remember and save. Did I listen? No. But I understand why my mom wanted me to learn that lesson and why it's necessary to save and build your credit wisely.

— Alan

I know I don't listen to this lesson much. I honestly don't think I have a "saving" bone in my body looking back on my life, but I know saving is so significant to you. So very important. Although I may be bad at it, I have always listened and put it in the back of my mind. I still hear you in my head screaming, "Save! Save! Save!" Although you sometimes think I am not, now I am. So thank you for that lesson.

— Alan

Leave a legacy of wealth through investments, insurance, real estate, and savings.

— Renny Jr.

3

Habits

S CHEDULES ARE ESSENTIAL TO ME, and I am gifted
at designing schedules to accomplish intended goals.
I can do 4 or 5 tasks at one time. I have learned over
the years that it is a gift to be able to schedule efficiently and
effectively. I believe I am good at this skill because I write down
everything I need to do, and I place it on a calendar. I can organize and implement big and little events from beginning to end.
I love it, and it is a gift. I am a person who likes to schedule.

Establishing a firm weekly work and family schedule kept us
on time and able to complete necessary daily tasks for everyone.
It also reduced uncertainty. Keeping the same consistent schedule every day and week establishes a habit. Established habits
help everyone do things without thinking. For example, daily
completing homework made it natural for the boys to complete
it without prompting.

Critical practices essential to helping their and my life move smoothly became something to practice; a habit. I wanted them to learn certain things I thought would be pleasurable for a woman to receive. For example, opening doors and pulling out chairs for women, providing compliments for nice things they observed about a woman or a fresh scent they smelled. We practiced daily. I never opened a door or pulled out my chair. It became a race to see which son would get to the door first. Speaking in complete sentences, walking tall, completing things you start, attending school every day, and church every Sunday are a few habits we established with our family. Today they all open doors for girls and women unless they refuse to let them.

Habits are hard to break and to create! Stephen Covey said, "It takes 21 days to create a habit." You will have much longer than 21 days. When you start early with your children practicing these relevant skills, they have seventeen years to practice with your coaching. Habits are hard to break. You want to establish appropriate habits because it is hard to correct learned habits. It takes forever to break a habit. To break a habit, you have to remember not to do it and then replace it with a new one. Think about losing weight. It takes forever to lose weight, but it takes minutes to gain it! Think about drinking soda and eating candy, lying, the expectation for getting good grades, respecting adults, and people. It takes forever to change a habit. Imagine letting your child mouth off or cuss at you for 21 days and then trying to correct it later after they became a high schooler. It will not happen without the consistency with which it started. Establishing a solid foundation early will benefit your family and community. Why are you practicing? Your life depends on it, and so does theirs. You can set them up to be distinguished for life.

My son Alan shared with me that your life maturation point stops at the age you do drugs. It is hard to break a drug habit because there is a certain amount of immaturity that exists. Alan shared that if you have been doing drugs since age 12, 15, 16 years old, etc., your maturity level is that age, even though you may be much older. Your reasoning level is also immature, so you may not think like a 30-year-old but a 12-year-old. So, when counselors try to help an individual understand the causes, consequences, and next steps to be successful, it is hard for that person to move because the behaviors and thoughts reflect the level of a 12-year-old.

I was amazed.

The more you learn, the more you grow. Building more concrete habits will shield the mind from the inappropriate behaviors that are all around us. I believe making a tough outer covering can prevent senseless mishaps. If I talked more pointedly about drugs, alcohol, and bad choices, it might have saved some of the pain my boys experienced. Instead, as a mother, I thought if it were not in their environment, it would not be a reason for them to experiment, but that was not realistic. Somehow, bad stuff will find its way into you and your children's lives. So doing all you can while you have them in your arms, in your home, will pave a way to help your children not step into a deep ditch.

How do you do teach this lesson?

List all essential habits:
- Sleep at a particular time.
- Body care (Wash face and body, brush teeth, brush hair/comb)
- Make bed
- Hang clothes in a specific place
- Homework (pencil, paper, computer, books, notebook, book bag) is the same time every day.

How will you see the lesson in practice?

- You will check every day. The hardest part is inspecting what kids do and when. Inspect what you expect. If you don't inspect, it will not get done. When you look things over, you provide feedback and coach them to perfect how they care for their bodies, make their bed, hang up their clothes, sit to do their homework, and seamlessly conduct themselves.

❧ **Notes from My Sons** ❧

Birds of a feather flock together!

If you sleep with dogs, you will wake up with fleas.

I learned this lesson early in my life. I remember my best friend in middle school was Kevin (called him O). We hung out all the time. When I started high school, Kevin went to another school. Kevin and his brother came to Eastmoor High School, where I attended school. I began to hang with Kevin and his brother, they were wild and out of control, but I loved it. As soon as I began to hang out with them., the principal was all over me. I was like, "Let me live, please." But she began to associate me with a different crowd. That moment in history taught me that if I hang with specific people, others will judge me according to their perception of those individuals.

It does not sound fair, but it's true. Thank God for this life lesson.

— Corey

4

Discipline

"Whoever spares the rod hates his son, but he who loves him is diligent to discipline him."

— Proverbs 13:24

WHEN MY GRANDDAUGHTER HARPER WAS two years old, she had a pen and went toward my white chest of drawers. I dashed across the bedroom, grabbed her pen, and said, "No." I looked her dead in her face with a firm eye, raised an eyebrow, and said, "You don't write on furniture. You write on paper."

Immediately, I changed the pen to a pencil and gave her a big sheet of paper. The moment she started writing on the paper, I praised her for following the directions and remembering to draw on the paper. I looked her dead in her face with a big smile and showed excitement about her remembering where to write.

Discipline is the means to teach or to learn. I work with many kids and adults, and I witness little discipline in a family or community. Instead, we give directions on where to go, what or not to get or do.

I imagine parents might be afraid or may not want to raise their kids the same way they were raised, although they turned out just right. I agree if damaging behaviors happened in your upbringing that brought physical, mental, and emotional damage, DO NOT REPEAT. But discipline is not that. When you teach, you are providing methods and strategies to increase their opportunity to get something right. For example, when Harper headed towards my chest of drawers, I redirected her. I didn't remove anything. I gave her an appropriate option.

I praised the correct behavior. If Harper went towards my furniture again, she would not be allowed to use the pencil because I would know she was not ready to follow my instructions by herself. I would give her a pencil but only in my presence. She wouldn't be allowed to sit and write without adult supervision.

Discipline is providing information and lessons to conduct one's life. Coach your child through the process so they won't forget. When kids are little, they don't know what to do. Please don't make assumptions about what you think they know. Consider if you didn't teach the lesson, your family doesn't know. Providing an array of teachings over many years, coupled with lots of practice, provides the foundation for making sound decisions. Remember, some students and adults require 1,400 practices to get it right.

How do you teach this lesson?

Discipline is teaching. Some teaching requires a spanking and a conversation. Others need a healthy discussion on what went wrong and what you expect. Some instructions may require the withholding of privileges.

A great lesson is around the expectations for completing homework or chores. My hubby told me his mom worked the second shift. His job was to wash and put the dishes away. If she returned home from work and the dishes weren't done, she would wake him or his brother out of their sleep to get it done. Does that inconvenience the parent? Yes! But it is for the ultimate good of the child. Discipline requires the student (child) to believe that you mean what you say. It requires the teacher (parent) to be consistent with monitoring what the child does. If the child does not follow through, the parent must provide the appropriate consequence or reward for the inappropriate or proper behavior.

How will you see it in practice?

- Kids follow through on what they are expected to do the first time. It means it is done the first time, immediately, or before you ask. If you find that it takes your child a long time to follow directions, give smaller tasks, things to do, or something that they could do and not fail. For example:
  1. Empty all trash cans every Sunday, Wednesday, and Friday.

2. Create a calendar that says trash days for Linda.

3. Go over the calendar.

4. Reminder to check the calendar for assignments, chores, or work.

5. Ask by repeating the day and the duties.

All these details are practice opportunities. Go to the calendar and check daily. Using the calendar allows children to practice calculating time, learning the days of the week and months of the year, and organizing themselves to complete tasks.

⊸♋ Notes from My Sons ♋⊸

Never be out of work or lazily do your job because you are un-focused. Always go the extra mile no matter how long it takes to accomplish a goal.

—Renny, Jr.

When I see this word, I think of focus. We focused on what you are currently doing and not getting distracted. Discipline is begin focused for a specified time on a specific task.

—Corey

You showed discipline in your work ethic, especially when you were getting your Ph.D. You tirelessly worked until it was perfect, or at least until it was right. It taught me a lot about what and how to get good grades and do well in school. I also think about family life. Dinner was on the table every night. We didn't sit in front of the TV. We sat at the table in the kitchen area, and we talked as a family. You came to all my shows and took me to all my auditions. While still maintaining friendships, relationships, and work. That's discipline as a parent, I think. And that's love overall.

—Alan

5

Resilience
(Never Give Up)

IVING AND GROWING UP IN a small city, I had opportunities to be involved in the town, community center, and church contests. As a result, I learned early on how to lose. Not academically, but socially. I would win some, but I placed 2nd or 3rd for many. Losing became second nature. I thought of losing as the next opportunity to try again or attempt a different contest. Losing never made me feel like a loser, or inadequate, or incapable of winning. It wasn't even an obstacle to stop me from trying multiple times. From these experiences, my ability to persevere during life challenges was more comfortable to manage because of the number of practices during my formative years of growing up.

Several years ago, I tutored a little boy. He had difficulty reading and felt very deflated. His fear of reading hampered him from trying other subject areas. The only thing he was not afraid of was a gigantic box of Legos. He could build anything. He loved to build Legos. But when he started coming to me, his heart was shattered, knowing that he could not read.

One time I was teaching him something he had never encountered before in school: multiplication. It was summer. When school started in the Fall, he would be a third-grader. Before he went back to school, I wanted him to be advanced in a content or subject area to allow him to shine and feel good about himself.

The moment I started teaching him how to solve multiplication problems, he told me he could never do that math. He screamed he didn't know it, and he wasn't smart enough to learn it. I immediately told him he was never allowed to say," "I can't!" In our home, words, and phrases like "I can't" were forbidden. I told him he didn't know how to do multiplication, YET, but he would know how before school started. His eyes got big. I held back tears and told him he would learn 4th-grade work early because he was smart enough to understand it. His life was never the same. He tried any and everything.

More than you could imagine, some individuals give up without trying because they are looking at the problem. I have seen many students give up before they start. They see a problem and assume they can't do it. Sometimes, it is hard for kids to comprehend that they may have skills to tackle a problem or question if they looked closely at it. Suppose they took the question apart and gave it 5 minutes of their time, then they might be able to work it out. I agree that some things are complex, but it does not mean you can't do them. For every single person, some things are complicated, and some things are easy. It is the way of life. So quitting is not an option. You cannot give up.

Life has taught so many of us that there is an ending date for all circumstances. Some come fast, but others take such a long time to end. I also learned that when the pain or obstacle becomes unbearable, the next moment is a win if you don't give up. You realize the power within after you stay the course. You build stamina by doing hard things, and when you finish, you understand something unique inside yourself—the power to go against your feelings and emotions. Every time our emotions get the best of us, they cause us to doubt the strength given to us to succeed. If our children learn when they are little to keep going until the whistle blows, they can conquer all things in front of them.

How do you build resilience? BY PRACTICE! If everything is easy, mapped out, or provided, there will be no way to build strength. Through practice, you can achieve skills and build character. I wish there was a wand you could wave, and everything we needed to know would enter into our minds. But it does not exist. All learning comes with practice.

What is hidden from most people is the amount of practice required to become great and successful. The home and family are essential because you have the time and opportunity to practice and not give up. Your loved ones can push you to stay in the game. This is true even for me. Just think, if Corey had not sent me pictures of completed books, encouraging me not to stop, this book might not be here. Just think, if my husband had not rallied around me and shared my dream with one of his clients, it might have taken me even longer to complete this book. Persistence is not a common practice.

I learned everyone must realize for themselves what they need to be successful. In graduate school, I knew I could be anything as long as I was willing to put in the time. Time and information are critical factors for success. I have worked harder during this season of my life than in the last couple of years of writing. I wrote four children's books, started a non-profit, and finished this book that you are reading. I didn't waste any time. At least 3-4 days out of the week, I got up like I was going out of the house to work. That meant there was not a lot of relaxation for me. I felt tired, but finishing these books was so important to me. I didn't want to stop until I finished. I could have created all kinds of excuses, but I refused to let our world's circumstances interrupt the one goal I wanted, a published book. I chose to make the best of this unusual time that G-d allowed.

Each of us must figure out how much energy, time, and re-sources are required to make our dreams come true. Once you have an idea, start and don't look back. Keep your goal in front and keep moving. I promise additional support, help, and con-fidence to finish will find their way to you if you stay the course and be persistent.

For example, to write a technically correct paper that is not about my feelings and thoughts, I would have to write and rewrite that paper at least 8-10 times. To master calculus or trigonome-try, it would take 1,400 practices. If I wanted to learn it, I would have to practice it that many times. I know what it takes. I know I have to take notes to understand most things and to remember them. If I don't take notes and recite the information repeatedly, I will not learn it.

Help your children see how they learn things, so they won't give up. Corey is an auditory learner. He learns by listening, and he listens to everything. Renny, Jr., and Alan are visual learners and can remember what they see. My daughter and friend Ugochi only watch shows and movies with subtitles. If there are no subtitles on a film, it is harder for her to grasp the meaning. Remember, no one waves a wand over our heads. The information or knowledge doesn't automatically appear. When you are sitting around with other people, it may seem like that happened, but it didn't. Practicing and not giving up makes you smart.

As a school administrator and working with kids in my home and community, I always made them repeat this phrase," "I will never give up!". Kids and adults often find themselves in situations that can cause them to avoid or not even try things. When detecting fear, I would ask," Are you giving up? Are you allowed to give up?"

My students always chanted, "I will never give up!"

How do you teach this lesson?

Help them understand what it takes to be successful at what they are doing. For example, some students can wake up the day of a spelling test and spell all words correctly on the spelling test, which means that the number of practices the teacher required at school was enough.

Some students have to write their spelling words down every night. The parent has to ask them to spell their words out loud and then write them down to get a 100% on the spelling test. So, if you knew that, you would do that every week and your child could get a 100%. If you don't want 100%, you won't practice that many times. You will settle for 70% or 80%, but it is not because your child is not intelligent or not capable. Because of the number of practices it takes to get 100%, they are unwilling to do so. Try providing only a few spelling words to practice on each day until the list is mastered.

Don't forget, some things are easy, and some things are hard. Spelling words may take a hundred practices, but math may take twelve. We have different skills. It will not all be the same for all things. Observing your family working and playing will help your child see what it takes for them to succeed. The more you practice, the stronger you get!

Finally, read stories to your children about resilience.

How will you see it in practice?

- You can see the evidence in your child's performance.
- You see them practice.
- You will see their willingness not to give up on small tasks and then a desire to try more complex problems.

~⊙ Notes from My Sons ⊙~

We will always encounter potholes called challenges in your life, but it is how you overcome adversity that shows you are a true leader.

—Renny, Jr

For Mother's Day this thank you message is a token of my love and appreciation for everything you. Thank you for being an amazing mom. I love you! I recognize and appreciate your immense contribution to my success, and I want you to know that I owe everything I have to you.

Remember, when we were young, and we had the early Saturday morning cleaning the house sessions before heading out to play my sports. Thank you! It has taught me in my 40's that persistence and the grind of executing business at a high level. This past Friday, I was talking with my barber, and he said, "Since I've known you for 20 plus years, you have been extremely focused person on your goals and never wavered. That is why your successful today because of your dedication to wanting to be great."

Thank you, mom; it's because of you that I can function and handle adversity when so many are killing themselves because of the grind of work and staying focused. I have been able to alleviate the stressors of leading teams because of your strength and teaching. Thank you for your prayers, not only me but Javonne and Sydney. Happy Mother's Day!

—Renny, Jr.

You taught me that all things are possible through God and God alone. That has built a foundation of spiritual resilience. I know that bad things happen to people, but if we truly trust in the Lord and believe His Word, we will make it through.

—Alan

Mom, I have seen you get knocked down and keep getting up! Resilience is going through something but not letting it beat you!

—Corey

6

Hard Work

RECENTLY, MY SISTA-GIRLFRIEND, DARCEL, AND I discussed my book *Doc's House*'s publication and the work that students put into afterschool tutoring. My students went to school all day and spent another 3 hours working after school. When they came to my house, they spent 45-60 minutes alone with me and then the remainder of their time completing work for review before leaving for home. When their work was done, they left. After school, tutoring occurred three days a week for most of the year. Think about this. My students were with me starting at age 3 ½. Over time, the students gained stamina and a great work ethic, but it took hard work for it to be achieved. They were going to school during the day and practicing more work after school. For seven years, these students sat with me to get smart.

Darcel and I discussed the type of strength these students

acquired over time. They worked extremely hard to get straight A's in school. Their classmates, teachers, and neighbors didn't know the amount of hard work they completed in advance to get straight A's in school. They probably thought they were just born smart. Nope. Each one of them worked hard to get smart. Because they are all different, some learned faster than others.

Students are discouraged in school because they work hard and can't see good grades. Parents, as their first coach, must help them make the right choices. Some kids will work hard at sports because they love it, but not their education, the thing they need the most. They won't exert the same effort in school or at home, but they will for something they love. School is sometimes hard to love because you can't see immediate results for your hard work. It is due mainly to not having the correct information to be successful.

It is possible to put in hard work and not achieve excellence— for example, athletes. They could practice and not win an event. It could be for several reasons: not catching or hitting a ball, not running fast, or jumping high enough. Those reasons are not because the athlete didn't stay after school every night and practice. The athlete may lack appropriate coaching to improve the technique or skill necessary to do well. All of these factors affect the hard work you put in. It doesn't matter how hard you work. If you don't have the correct technique or know the right information, you will fail every time. So you might get disappointed because your hard work is not paying off. It didn't make you smarter or better. I encourage you to help your kids, your teams, spouses, and friends have early wins.

Home is the place to practice hard work. You and your family can practice difficult skills or chores correctly. I encourage you to practice the things you hate the most. Find and post a picture of the way it should look when it is finished. Schools don't teach hard work. They don't go over the meaning of hard work or how to do it. They believe it is the parent's job, and as parents, we think the school will instill it in our kids. But schools don't teach these principles. They hope each kid will enter the classroom with a desire to work hard.

Human beings need a reason to believe in themselves. Home is the best place to instill greatness by showing and helping your child experience hard work, so it becomes a natural desire. Sometimes these lessons are hard to teach because they require a great effort on the parent's part. It requires you to monitor and provide small tasks or jobs for your family to complete. As the small steps are mastered, you add more. Complete a five-minute practice every day so you don't feel overwhelmed. It equals 35 minutes of practice in a week, 140 minutes of practice in a month, and 1,680 minutes in a year. Now multiply that by 12 years. Shouldn't you see greatness? Just think if you did a five-minute practice here and there for everything. Just five minutes!

How do you teach this lesson?

Give your child something hard to do. Coach them through the process. I watched kids not be able to sweep a floor because they never held a broom. So cleaning the floor was hard. They could finish the floor and still see trash and look confused about why it was still there. Show them how to wash dishes and then check. Many things are about coaching to complete the task and make it perfect.

How will you see it in practice?

- Tasks are completed without crying and whining. Kids or young adults finish without complaining.
- Your child will stay up late to finish an assignment or chore without grumbling.
- Your child will decide they cannot play with their friends because they have work to do.
- They will ask for assistance or help to do something thoroughly or correctly.

❧ Notes from My Sons ❧

Always remember nobody owes you anything, so you must fight for everything you want. But most importantly, if you stay sold out for God, it makes your fight a lot easier. God has great things in store for so stay committed to the process, and you will come out victorious.

—Renny, Jr.

Love your passions because it comes from God. Never waver from what God has planned for you because God will reroute you back to where he prepared for you to be. It just depends on how long you want it to take to see what great things he has in store.

—Renny, Jr.

Better late than never! You are the one who I first thought was crazy for having more than one job. But this must be the new craze because everyone is doing it. Every older person I know has all these different side jobs. The hustle is real to keep the lifestyle you want. I'm upset that I learned it at an older age. But one needs more than one job to survive unless they are making $20 million a movie. So, thank you for that lesson.

—Alan

7

Responsibility/ Accountability

*A*LONG WITH HARD WORK ARE responsibility and accountability for your words, work, and actions. I recently heard a YouTube sermon from Andy Stanley. When he went to high school, he had no rules. He shared that his parents felt like they had given him enough information about the Lord and taught him to be fully accountable to God for everything that happened in his life. He shared with the audience that his parents refrained from giving him advice. They told Andy to seek the Lord. I was so intrigued by their parenting. How could parents create this type of accountability in a high school student? Then I thought about home as the practice run for the rest of one's life. We are instilling in our kids our family's characteristics and values to last a lifetime.

If kids don't know accountability, it can wreck their lives. You are preparing each child or young person to live or work with other people. Your work can equip them to understand and be accountable for their actions and their behavior towards others. If you could do what you wanted at any time and no one could question you, you would have a hard time at work, at play, and in relationships. When responsibility and accountability are developed, it positively impacts how we move in our communities, in school, and at home.

Home is the best place to instill greatness by helping children experience hard work, so it becomes a natural inclination. You don't wake up desiring to work hard. You wake up trying to figure out how not to work hard, how to skimp, how to make half of the bed, mow some of the grass, how to pick up some of the leaves, and half wash the dishes mainly because there is no accountability on the part of the one watching. I remember one of my cousins only ironed the part of the shirt people could see. I couldn't believe it!

How do you teach this lesson?

Have your child write out their weekly chores and responsibilities. Please post it on the refrigerator or somewhere they can easily view and refer back to it.

How will you see it in practice?

- You will see the work done on the date/time it should be done.
- Your child will refer back to the weekly chore/responsibility list or mention their tasks throughout the week.

~~ Notes from My Sons ~~

A man should always have some money in his pocket!
It's so crazy sometimes when I think of all the things that should stick with me but did not stick at all. My mom tried to teach me so many things that I did not let sink in my head. (Most things did)

I remember this day clearly. On my way to school, my mom stopped me and asked if I had any money in my pocket.

I said, *"No, I did not have any money."*

She said, *"Corey, a man should always have something in his pocket. What if you ran out of gas or someone needed something?"*

It made so much sense to me! She then gave me a few dollars and sent me on my way to school. Then, I thought to myself, *"This can't be enough money."*

From that moment on, I always tried to keep money in my pocket. I want to think that throughout my 32 years, I have done well with this life lesson.

—Corey

Save, Invest, and Grow your money.
This is an exciting concept. Since I was in elementary school, I have been doing this when my dad opened up my first bank account. I remember to this day when my dad and I went to US Bank and opened up that account. I think I even had a couple of hundred dollars to place in that account that day. Most people that know me understand that I am serious about my money. I hope to continue to make significant investments with my money. So one day, the money I saved will be enough to do great things for the people I love.

—Corey

8

Your Word/
Trust/Truth

OW DO YOU BUILD TRUST? When I was a little girl, the 6th grade class graduated from elementary school and went to junior high school (7th – 9th grade in my education era). My dad told me that I would receive a new dress. The time was fast approaching, and I asked my dad for my dress. He pulled his pocket inside out and said he had no money to get me a dress.

I asked him, "Did you lie to me? You told me you would get me a dress."

Well, as you can tell, I have never forgotten that moment. That moment left an impressionable mark in my brain and my heart. My dad's words to me provided an invaluable lesson. I used that lesson to guide my actions and behaviors with all people, specifically my kids. I never told them anything I would do that I didn't do. I didn't make promises that I didn't keep. The experience with my dad made me honor my word.

My word means everything to me. I think before I make a promise. I examine my pocket, resources, and time before telling someone what I can or cannot do.

When you work with kids, which I have done my entire career, when you say something is due or state a consequence or promise a reward, kids are watching. Adults are watching. Honor it, or they will never let you forget it.

Kids will trust what you do and not what you say. Kids know when you lie. Simple incidents like promising an ice cream cone, watching a movie with them, fixing their hair, throwing the ball outside, or taking them over grandma's can cause mistrust. All these unkept promises add up to be big things over time. Your word and trust are established by what you say and do.

Kids must also demonstrate their ability to be trusted. As kids become more independent, it is essential to rely upon what they say and do. Their lives depend on how much you can believe them. Curfews, completing chores, and being in the right place are excellent examples of building trust. When kids follow your directions and follow-through, they are honoring you. Enforce telling the truth and not lying.

My son Corey will not lie. He will stay silent in order not to lie. It is fascinating to watch him as an adult, choosing his words carefully not to lie. While Corey lived in the city, we spent countless hours having in-depth mom and son times at mealtime. It was one of my most memorable and cherished times. We would sit and catch up about our life. In his voice, I could hear how he carefully framed how he answered a question so that he could never be caught lying. I would chuckle, thinking, "That question is off-limits." or "He is not ready to divulge his true feelings about that."

Demand that kids tell the truth. Now, I say this with great caution. As an adult, your behavior will need thorough examination because it is hard to speak to a child or anyone in your family with the saying, "Do as I say and not I as do." The old folks used that as a favorite phrase, but that does not work today. Building and establishing trust takes a while, but it can be broken and damaged quickly. Helping a child at an early age be trustworthy allows for greater independence later at the right time. As children mature and the trust level between you and them increases, more autonomy can be granted.

How do you teach this lesson?

Ask the questions often and listen for the correct answer (especially on things you know the right solution to) so you can hold children accountable. Have a village of people/ support of others who can confirm what kids have or have not done. Ask others to verify the truth.

How will you see it in practice?

- Your child repeats the rule/reason behind telling the truth.
- Your child will tell you the truth.

~~ **Notes from My Sons** ~~

Do what you say you would do. Your word is your bond. All you have is your word.

—Corey

I feel like this was just always ingrained in me since day one. To tell the truth and do what I say, I would do. It wasn't until I left home that this theme left me in a way. But growing up, we could always trust what you said and trust that you wouldn't lie to us. Everything you said you did. If you didn't – you would say you couldn't. Or surprise us with it in the end.

—Alan

Trust yourself and live your truth. God has a plan for you, so trust in God with all your mind, body, and soul.

—Renny, Jr.

9

Independence

*A*s I was writing this section, somehow, I remembered that my mom let me go out at 16 years old. The only rule she stated was our curfew. We had to be home by eleven during the week and by midnight on the weekends. There were no other rules. She had firmly established school, work, extracurricular activities, and chore expectations, even early morning for Sunday School and church. She rarely asked about my whereabouts or what I needed or wanted. My brother and I were free to go. She trusted us to do the right thing, and we did.

As a result of being raised in that manner, my boys experienced a similar upbringing and independence. Early in our family, I established curfew, church, schoolwork, extracurricular activities, and work expectations. All of my sons' actions were monitored throughout their growing up. I granted independence as they proved they could continuously make sound decisions and do the right thing when I was not watching. My sons' actions guided me in giving more or less. My children earned the right to freedom.

Independence is earned, not granted because you are a certain age. You would hope that kids could drive when they turn 16 years old. But if they have proven to be reckless, unable to make sound decisions, or cannot respect authority, do not give them keys. As I observed my kids, I watched their ability to follow directions the first time, their willingness to listen, and their ability to ask questions and desire help. I have been fortunate, and this does not happen for all kids, to give more independence as they met the age milestones only because these boys never gave me an ounce of trouble. They did some naughty things growing up at home, but nothing that warranted me having to lock them down. I feel very blessed because when parents are separated, it can produce problems, specifically for the mother.

How do you teach this lesson?

Monitor and setting appropriate and flexible ranges of freedom. Create if/then agreements or statements.

How will you see it in practice?

- When you monitor the freedoms, they will successfully be able to handle them. Various privileges can be increased in increments.

~❧ Notes from My Sons ❧~

You allowed us to let you make your own decisions, and at times it created bad mistakes for us, but it has groomed us into the people we are today.

—Renny, Jr.

Mom forced independence on me. I can remember the moment freedom (and it wasn't even that big) happened for me. When you told me I would have to pay for my cell phone bill. Oh, I was so upset. I was more in fear than anything – the fear I wouldn't have enough money or fear that this was too much responsibility as I had just graduated college and, you know, poor me. When in actuality, it was something that needed to happen. If you didn't – I would probably let you pay for the next five years. But instead, you had confidence in me and knew it was time.

—Alan

I remember you leaving us at home alone and putting that trust in us to do what was right. You would either be gone on a work trip and made sure we had food for each day. I think that taught us independence in a way. I was not sure how legal that was, but it taught me to take care of myself without a parental figure around. Or when you let me go to the Broadway shows on my own as you and my brothers' shop. I truly appreciated that. I was still in my element, and you put that trust and faith that I would be okay. I remember the big one when we stayed near the New York airport, and I wanted to go to a show in the city. You put me in a cab. You couldn't afford for both of us to go. I was scared. I'm not sure you could tell, but you let me go. But that risk you took was all I needed for me to believe in myself. But that's important for parents and people in a relationship. Take that risk and put it all on God to do what he does best, protect His loved ones.

—Alan

10

Health/Exercise

*M*Y FATHER WAS FROM CHICAGO. I stayed in
Chicago during the summer many times. I explic-
itly remember visiting my grandmother, auntie,
and cousin two times a year. My father's sister was at least 500lbs
or more. As a child, I knew I would have to exercise. As I write
this, it is incredible the kind of impressions that stayed with me.
If I did not exercise, I would look like my aunt, and I couldn't. So
as a child, I ran in the park daily. As an adult, I did aerobics five
days a week before going to work. I walked four miles in the park
before heading to work, or I worked out in my home. I had train-
ers, and I learned to love exercise due to the fear of being huge. My
children's dad ran every day too, but he was also an athlete.

Establishing and learning healthy practices early is critical.
My two oldest boys always played sports, so exercise was second
nature. Corey decided after playing sports that exercise was not

essential until he found health issues that caused him to go back to exercise. Alan, my youngest, despised sports and did not exercise until his 30's.

Overall, healthcare, as well as exercise, is essential. I knew that African-American men died at an alarming rate, and research indicated they were less likely to go to the doctor. So I prioritized and made the annual doctor visits an experience. I taught my sons to share all concerns with their doctor. I prompted them to ask questions in front of the doctor. How did they feel? Did they have any concerns about their heart, head, or body? Any concerns about their penis or underarms? I wanted them to know that it was a place to inquire about their health needs. I made this a BIG deal! I didn't want them to be afraid but fearless about developing a culture of healthy living.

I still believe it today.

How do you teach this lesson?

Present activities (such as walking with your kids, playing outside) for 30 minutes – 1 hour. Start with 15 minutes and gradually increase the range of time to build up stamina.

How will you see it in practice?

- Kids will automatically begin the activities and encourage you and others to participate.

❧ Notes from My Sons ☙

Eat healthily, work out, and stay in shape!
Your body is your temple! Do not ruin the one body you get in life. Take care of your body because one day you may need it!

—Corey

As a black man, you have to be mentally, physically, and spiritually to fight daily challenges.

—Renny, Jr.

11

Communication – Talking, Listening Skills & Technology

*T*EACHING YOUR CHILD THE ART of communicating will be essential in this day and age. I believe some technology hampers our practice with verbal conversations, meaning that it may take longer for a child or teen to learn this critical skill. Speaking clearly and distinctly is understood through years of practice. Saying the entire word and not leaving off the endings to words are so important to me. Looking the person in the eye when you are talking to them is an indicator of respect and listening. It also allows the speaker to gauge whether or not you understand what they are telling you. Practice asking your child: "What did I say?" and "What do you understand?".

My son Alan hated having to repeat what he learned at church. I wanted to make sure he was listening and that there were no misconceptions about what he heard.

Reviewing Sunday's sermon was also an opportunity to practice speaking and communicating their thoughts and feelings. Dialoguing with your children helps them develop the skill to participate in conversations. It reduces their fear of participating in discussions. You can help them to learn how to listen and respond timely to others. You can help your children know how to contribute to the discussion and not feel discouraged if someone does not agree. They can grow to understand how people have opinions rooted in facts and experiences—some important things to teach.

The shared conversation comes from preparation. Don't you hate when people want to add something to the discussion, and it has nothing to do with what you are talking about? Help the ones you love to develop their talking points around information that is factual and relevant.

Teach your children not to interrupt people when they are talking. I have a friend who consistently works to finish your sentence or thoughts. She wants you to know that she has the answer. It is very unpleasant when it happens so frequently, and she knows it. When that happens, I stop talking and wait for her to finish. She blames it on having five other siblings. With so many siblings, she had to fight to get her thoughts across. "UMMM," I say, "But it is disrespectful."

Additionally, help your children eliminate "Yeah," "Huh?" "What?" and "Nope" from their vocabulary. Have them replace those words immediately by speaking in complete sentences.

My children were never allowed to participate in conversations with adults. Try to prevent them from growing up too fast or thinking that they are an adult. My mom raised me to understand that kids played with kids entirely. Kids can't handle information or know how to use it properly. Monitor your language. Kids hearing concerns and issues can stress them out and cause them to feel adult burdens without you being aware.

In a relationship, it is essential to know what a person is honestly saying. My husband may be trying to formulate his thinking to say something the right way. It is his pet peeve. He does not want anything to come out of his mouth the wrong way. He will walk away and say, "I am thinking how to say it."

I say, *"Okay!"*

Additionally, there should be no penalty for sharing your thoughts in the rules of engagement, no degrading or laughing at views that are different unless someone makes a joke. But a person's looks, language, expressions, or thinking cannot be the target of your jokes. The family is not the place to put someone you love on display through sarcasm or ridicule. It was a law in my house that you could not talk about or make fun of people. They could not see people on the street and have an unkind word to say about them. They were not allowed to use people of any kind, color, or size as the brunt of their jokes or tolerate it in their company.

A cell phone can be helpful, but it can lead to misuse and abuse. Another part of good communication is turning it off when you are in the company of adults or setting it on vibrate. If you are going to work or an interview, turn it off.

If you need to have it on, share that you will be receiving a call from your parents or job. Then leave the room, talk, and return as quickly as possible. It isn't polite to take and make calls when you are with your friends and family for a designated period. Ignoring your company to talk on the phone shows your friends and family disrespect and that you have forgotten your manners.

At the dinner table, I established a "no cell phone" rule. We would have family dinner once a month. The cell phones dinged, eyes were focused on the keypads, and no one paid attention to the people at the table. I couldn't take it. I honored the attendance of my guest and family. I wanted it to be a time to talk and catch up on our lives. Banning the cell phone at the table became non-negotiable.

Listening, not interrupting a person, using manners when having a cell phone, and making eye contact during a conversation are critical skills to develop and demonstrate to others how you respect them.

How do you teach this lesson?

Ask a question and see how your children answer.

1. Do they answer in complete sentences?
2. Do they look you in the eye when they speak?
3. How is their body language?
4. Do they answer the question?
   a. Do they understand the question? Note: Children should not be afraid to say that they don't know the

answer. Help them learn how to ask the person speaking to repeat the question differently.

b. Have your child practice answering and asking questions.

How will you see it in practice?

- The kids will say, "I don't know" or "What does that mean?" "I don't understand."
- Kids will be more confident in their ability to communicate.

~ **Notes from My Sons** ~

As a kid watching you work in the classroom or at seminars taught me the valuable lesson of catching the room's attention. You command the room when you speak. You have this light, if I should say, that radiates off you when you talk. Every head turns, and that's what I try to grasp when I am in a room full of people. There has to be this radiance or glow that gets brighter and brighter but doesn't blind. I use this skill in acting and managing people. I'm trying to heighten this aspect of myself so that people pay attention. It's all because of you. So I am thankful for that lesson.

—Alan

12

Posture

STANDING TALL AND SITTING TALL is a learned behavior. Kids don't automatically learn to sit tall. Sitting or walking with your back firm and straight is learned. When children lay down to write, talk, or eat, it rubs me so wrong. Why? First of all, it is laziness. What prevents you from sitting and standing tall? It is not healthy for your back. I see so many adults in a meeting, with elbows on the table, one hand holding up one side of their face while trying to talk. It is hard for you to understand them clearly, and it appears that they are exhausted. In virtual settings, it is worse. You see adults and kids leaning over the chair, feet on the table, curled up, or flopped over on a desk. You can barely pay attention to their words because their posture is so disruptive. Their fingers are in their mouth. They're chewing on their tongue and pulling on their clothes or hair. Practice walking, standing, and sitting tall with your kids. Teach them to look like they own the room. Provide reminders, prompt them to pick up their feet and not slide across the room. Teach them not to slouch. I know it seems crazy, but your appearance and attitude are the first part of the battle to getting in the door. Don't let your appearance be the reason you can't walk through.

How do you teach this lesson?

Remind kids to sit up. Ask them not to put their heads on the table. Ask your child to walk straight and not hunched. Show your children pictures of people who have poor posture versus those with good posture. Have children sit in the middle of their chair (not using the back of your chair as a resting spot) and plant their feet on the floor. If your child sits towards the end of the chair, it forces one to sit up.

How will you see it in practice?

- Your child will display good posture, or they will self-correct poor posture.
- As your child learns to sit, they can sit towards the back of the chair.

∼ **Notes from My Sons** ∼

Sit up and eat the right way.

— Renny, Jr.

Sit up straight!

— Corey

The dreaded posture. In the church, you always had that hand sliding down our backs when we were slouching. Or we would have to sit at the edge of the chair. It sometimes was frustrating as I didn't see other kids have to deal with posture, but I'm grateful for it today. I do sit remarkably better than some.

—Alan

13

Manners

URING A VISIT TO SEE my brother in California, my great-niece and nephew came to Sunday dinner with their parents. All the kids were seated at the kid table. While I served dessert, I engaged them in a conversation about school, things they liked, and their dreams. They astounded me with their eye contact. They faced me, addressed me as Auntie, and answered the questions. They didn't put their heads down or say "Ummm," "I dunno," or gaze into the sky. To capture my attention with their focus on me, they consistently used the words, "Yes, please!" and "Yes, thank you!" or "No, thank you"!" They never missed a beat. I was shocked. I worked with kids all the time, and I never heard or saw kids speak pleasantly, directly, and with confidence without prompting. I asked my niece Tasha if she taught her children to respond in that manner.

TEACHABLE MOMENTS   91

She said, "No, but we always say please and thank you, yes ma'am or no ma'am."

Her response confirmed for me that behavior consistently modeled teaches children how to behave and respond to others. Even when we don't talk, we are teaching. Our values are displayed daily in how we interact with others in our home and at work. Our values are on display, whether intentional by words or by what we do.

Manners melt the heart of men and women. Alan worked for a high-end hotel in New York. One day, as I waited for him to finish his shift, I watched him greet his customers as they came in. He greeted them by their name and ended his registration with, "It has been my pleasure to serve you, Mr. ...."

I learned from him to say, "It is indeed my pleasure."

Taking a few moments to make eye contact and say, "thank you" and their name or "please" and their name with your request, will position you ahead of everyone around you. People, especially adults, will react to you differently. They will take notice of your manners and tell others about you.

Also, quickly apologize and admit when you are wrong. Don't justify it. Immediately admit what you did because everyone makes mistakes. While you are practicing skills and lessons, you will make more mistakes than you want. As you mature and learn, you will make fewer mistakes, and you remember the things that caused you to say you were sorry. I love my husband because he is so quick to say, "You are right. I am wrong." He doesn't try to say, "I wanted to" or " I wish I could have," "You know I was too busy to," or "Why didn't you remind me to do it?"

He says, "I am sorry. I was wrong. I never want you to be unhappy."

I melt. My mouth closes, and I have nothing more to say. When kids experience true forgiveness for wrongdoing and genuinely realize that all people make mistakes, they will quickly apologize and plan to do the right thing.

How do you teach this lesson?

Choose keywords and phrases that children can frequently apply (such as: thank you, welcome, please). Encourage eye contact when speaking to anyone. Remind your child to apologize quickly when a mistake is made and not justify why. But remember not to do it again.

At mealtime, teach your child to chew with their mouth closed and not to talk with food in their mouth. Before your child eats, teach them to thank the person (people) who have provided their meal. Teach them also to wait until everyone's meal is served before they begin eating.

Teach your child not to interrupt when someone is speaking (even when it comes to siblings or other children). Teach them to wait to be acknowledged before speaking. (At school, children should raise their hands and wait.) Teach your child to knock and wait for an invitation before entering a room. Teach your child to write a note to say thank you.

How will you see it in practice?

- Automatic use of keywords and phrases
- Your child will close their mouth when they eat.
- Self-correcting their interruptions and wait to be acknowledged before speaking.

Notes from My Sons

Being kind is one of the more vital attributes I received from you. Another good and bad trait, you could say. Some say I'm too kind, and I believe that. But I can't help it. I like to see the joy in people's eyes or want to see a smile come to someone who was having a bad day. I love to make sure people are happy, and if that means I must listen to them vent for 30 minutes or if I have to spend my last $5 to get them a drink, then so be it as long as I know they won't go home and do something stupid with their lives. You showed me that when you have those teachable moments with me or you made me feel special when you always answered my phone calls. You showed me when you kicked me out of the room when you were having a grown-up conversation – of course, I still listened, but I knew that it was something profound that you had to listen to and be there for someone. You radiate kindness. You radiate goodness. Thank you for that lesson.

—Alan

14

Consequences

ONE THING THAT I LEARNED as I have aged is that consequences impact the family and community. We can experience unexpected effects by just being a family member. When a family member is hurt, someone has to be responsible for their kids until they get well. When your parent tells you don't play in the street and you do it anyway, you get hurt. You then miss school. Your parents miss work. You can't finish playing ball for school, and now you miss out on a scholarship. Consequences.

The most prominent public display of receiving consequences for actions was viewing the police's activity on the death of Mr. George Floyd. I know the nation would have never imagined that his death would cause worldwide attention, outcry, and change. One horrible decision caused the entire country to finally see firsthand police injustice against people of color, followed by peaceful protests, police policy changes, and personnel removal.

When opportunities present themselves, thoroughly explain that one wrong move can cause life to change drastically. I taught my youngest son how to drive. We were in a parking lot, and I explained the importance of using side-view mirrors and looking out of his window for cars. He quickly told me he could see, knew what to do, and didn't need those mirrors. So, I stopped him abruptly and angrily talked about individuals' lives on the street and how one wrong move could change his life.

I told him a story of a man who accidentally hit a child. He was in an SUV, and the kid ran out in front of him while he pulled off from the curb. He had no way of knowing that the kid was there. It wasn't his fault, but he never forgave himself for the mistake and spent the rest of his life on drugs trying to reduce the memory of what happened. I shared that story with him at that moment. I explained that all the mirrors were there to help prevent him from the chance of making an unforgivable mistake. I told him about looking out for the blind spot. I knew that a wrong decision would not only impact him but me and everyone connected to me. It would be raise the cost of my insurance. He may even end up in jail. I made a big deal because I could weigh the cost, and he couldn't. He didn't have the experience or the knowledge to know the impact of one wrong decision.

When kids don't do right the right thing, they don't know the consequence. Help them understand that you can receive rewards for every good act, but every wrong decision, either big or small, always has an unknown impact on the people in your surroundings. That is what is scary about life. You are not guaranteed the result you expected. Sometimes, we think we escaped, so we continue down the wrong path. Then suddenly, our world comes crashing down hard on us. The lesson on consequences is an important lesson to drill in your kids to prevent a crash. A hiccup is different than a crash and a fire. Fires and collisions can take our children out of the game for an extended period. Why? Because they had no idea the consequence, and no one explained it. Doing wrong for some kids is fun and adventurous. We have all been kids. Some bad things are just fun to do, like a missing curfew. I don't mean life-threatening things, but something that won't kill you, you hope. Missing curfew could put you in the wrong place at the wrong time, and it could cost you your life.

Today there are cameras everywhere but make no mistake that the G-d we serve sees everything. There is no escape from His power or actions. He gives excellent whispers and warnings before He cuts loose on His children. That is a perfect point to tell our children. They want your discipline because The Father in heaven is next, and they should be concerned because He knows the future. You don't.

How do you teach this lesson?

Consistently implement appropriate consequences so children know the importance of behavior. For example:

1. When a child misses curfew, shorten curfew time.
2. When a child misses checking in with you while traveling to school/etc., limit phone privileges.

3. When a child abuses phone privileges, limit or remove phone privileges.
4. When a child neglects chores, set a specific date and time (at inconvenience to child) where you can monitor your child's progress.

How will you see it in practice?

- When you ask your child to do something, they do it. As you coach them, decrease or increase the boundary limits as you see your child consistently meeting those expectations.

~ **Notes from My Sons** ~

I'm not sure I got in trouble enough to have severe consequences growing up. I remember having to sit at the dinner table if we couldn't summarize the sermons at church, but I don't think I categorized that as a consequence. Those were more lessons than anything because it left me feeling that I had to do better at listening next time. The only severe consequence was in College when I totaled my car, and I thought you would get me a new car. But you nipped that in the bud real quick.

—Alan

If you do wrong, expect bad. If you do good, expect good. There is a consequence for every action. You get what you give!

—Corey

Understand right from wrong because you will end up in places you don't want to be.

—Renny, Jr.

15

Reflections

*H*OW ADULTS CONDUCT THEMSELVES INSIDE their home serves as a model for acting outside the home. As a teacher, I often wondered how kids knew inappropriate words or would say demeaning things to adults. After a while, it became clear that kids modeled what they saw and heard in their environment. One day my girlfriend Martha was in our home, and she noted, "You guys are so polite to one another."

I said, "What do you mean?"

She told me most married couples didn't treat each other with kindness or with manners.

Soft skills such as communication, posture, and health are traits to be diligent in teaching. Respect, integrity, and independence are essential ingredients in building strong character and a foundation for growing strong roots. Take moments to reflect on your actions, how you treat each other, ways to improve to be more productive and be an example for others to model. Your reflection time is also an opportunity to remember that you are building amazing people to be with others. Your coaching not only helps your child individually, but your child's actions will help an entire community thrive from home to work and school.

How do you teach this lesson?

Set aside some time (weekly, bi-weekly, etc.) for your child to reflect on their behavior and adult/parent behavior. Use this time to speak about specific positive things that your child has seen and then have them say or develop ways to improve.

How will you see it in practice?

- Kids will want to meet or remind you of your meeting.
- Kids could write their thoughts or collect thoughts in a jar and pull them out (review) during the scheduled meeting.

~ಲ **Notes from My Sons** ಲ~

Always reflect and give yourself time to relax, sit back, evaluate and find areas in your life to improve. Continuously strengthen your strengths and build up your weaknesses.

—Renny, Jr.

You were a big one about reflections, mostly on ourselves and on you. Through your yearly letters, you would have us write about the lessons we learned from you. Or our dinner conversations about our day, there would always be an element of reflective lessons. When the new year would come around, I remember us talking about our goals and what we wanted to do in the upcoming year. But the thing about your reflections is that they taught me about growth (within myself and each other), and they allowed us to see the perspective from outside ourselves when we talked about it as a family.

—Alan

16

Personal Hygiene and Cleaning up After Yourself

WHEN CHILDREN GROW UP, THEIR bodies change. Parents often notice before the child that there is a body odor. If you want other kids and adults to desire to be in their company, showering and brushing teeth is non-negotiable. Parents can help by reminding kids early in their stage of life about the critical areas on their bodies they have to wash daily such as underarms and private parts, as well as often neglected areas like behind the ears, the navel, between the toes, and ankles. Teach them the importance of soap and deodorant and not wearing too much cologne or perfume.

Keeping a clean body and wearing clean clothes can take a long time to teach. I encourage you to start early and make it a fun time, especially bath time. Teaching children about their appearance and cleanliness is an opportunity for kids to give a good first impression.

For girls, teach them not to use makeup to destroy their beauty or use makeup to make them into somebody else. Also, I love Vaseline and Hydrogen Peroxide. Hydrogen Peroxide is a very cheap way to kill bad breath, infection and keep your teeth white. I asked a dentist one time what the #1 toothpaste was? She recommended Hydrogen Peroxide and baking soda. All I know is Hydrogen Peroxide and Vaseline are my staples. Vaseline is for every ashy kneecap, elbow, heel, leg, arm, and thigh.

Practicing daily personal hygiene habits are essential to do no matter what happens in the world or how unimportant it may seem. It is hard to break bad habits. Perfecting practice with personal care will last all the days of their life. So, practice the right way. Practice being ready so you never have to get prepared.

BEDROOMS, BATHROOMS, SHARED SPACE, AND KITCHENS

Alan thanked me recently for teaching cleanliness. He has roommates who have a difficult time picking up after themselves in a shared space. He gets so irritated. Teach your children the importance of how to clean their room, bathroom, and common areas.

Most of the time, we tell our children to clean their room or clean up the kitchen. We assume they know what we mean. I encourage you to think in this way. You know how you want an area to look. Let this be a teachable moment. Show them. Then coach them through completing the task independently.

It is essential to coach our kids and loved ones through learning how to do something. If you see yourself as a coach, then it is a win for them and you if they are successful. If they aren't successful, change your strategy for their success. Don't forget some people need more practice. The more we practice the correct way, the better we get. Remember, you are on a team called "Family." The team is successful because of the team members. You want a winning team, not just winning individuals.

How do you teach this lesson?

Show your child the steps it takes to complete a chore/task and coach them through these tasks. For example: making the bed or washing dishes. Show your child how to clean the crucial areas of their bodies and the ones often forgotten.

How will you see it in practice?

- A child will complete a chore/task independently how you taught them (or in a new or improved way).
- A child will monitor their body odor or appearance and take the necessary steps to ensure they are presentable.

‹ Notes from My Sons ›

Cleaning both home and self-cleaning is essential to a healthier life.

—Renny, Jr.

Take pride in your appearance. Take care of the things you have.

—Corey

We had to clean our house every Saturday morning.

—Alan

Part III

Life Lessons

"Give, and it will be given to you. A good measure, pressed down, shaken together, and running over, will be poured into your lap. For with the measure you use, it will be measured to you."

— LUKE 6:38

"But my G-d shall supply all your need according to His riches in glory by Christ Jesus."

— PHILIPPIANS 4:19

"Now He who supplies seed to the sower and bread for food will also supply and your store of seed and will enlarge the harvest of your righteousness."

—2 CORINTHIANS 9:10

1

Give

*G*IVING REQUIRES THAT YOU PAY attention to the people you love and care about and the community in which you live. Teaching giving requires that you help your child take note of the things people like and do. Sharing your resources and time is easier when you know something about the people you love. Keeping notes on the places they go, their activities and entertainment experiences, foods they like to eat, beverages they drink, and the pressing community causes or concerns they address will make it easier for you to find things to give to them. Giving is expressed in the thought you provide in selecting or creating the gift. It will give the receiver immense joy.

When I was a principal, I worked in an impoverished school. My students were encouraged to give. Even in our poverty, it is vital to think of others. We would raise money during the holiday season by bringing any loose coins to give to children less fortunate than ourselves. We collected money and took it to the radio station to put with their money to provide toys and food for families. When the radio station announced our school as a donor to help kids and families, pride and humbleness swept through our school and community. We were overjoyed, and it caused us to do more.

The students thought about other ways to make a difference and to care. We found other projects to do in our community. We wrote letters for the elderly to their families. We performed our Christmas concert in their facilities. We baked cookies and read stories to the elderly who had no families. Finally, we found that giving was contagious, not just for the community, but we found a place in our hearts to treat the students and adults around us with kindness. As a result of our commitment to taking care of our community, Renny Jr., Corey, and Alan make us proud of their work to help others and the community. When you care, the other person's needs drive your action. Giving is something to cherish.

Giving can never be seen as loaning or bartering. Loaning and bartering are based on a time frame and receiving something in return. I will provide you with this for this. Some people are not givers. They don't believe in it. Try hard to remove yourself from that environment. It can become toxic. In an environment of givers, everyone gives at different or exact times. But when you are around takers, they don't replenish the group or the earth. They take until everything is gone, and then they move on to the next group. I generally do not linger with takers because I recognize the damage they can do. They strip you down and not only take your physical items, but they aim for bigger things like your heart and soul. Women are often caught in relationships like this because we are generally compassionate and kind. We are so diligently giving that we miss signs of the other person not giving.

In the light of this information, your family must recognize and pay attention to people in their surroundings. Help them understand that some people work hard to harm and not to do good. It is the nature of our society, and we are not exempt from those experiences. But if we help our children be conscious of how often their friends share a coke, a piece of candy, purchase or create birthday or Christmas gifts, the list of friends might get short. The awareness of specific behaviors to indicate whether or not a person cares is the lesson you want to instill in your child. Be observant and don't assume a person can't give because they cannot afford it. There are thousands of ways to show you care that doesn't cost money. Giving is not buying the attention or love of another. Give just because you want to. Nothing else. When I had little to give in my lean years, I would pray and ask for more to give more. The Lord always showed up, and He has given me more to offer.

Recently, I was at my son's home with his family.

He said, "Mom, I know that we cannot beat G-d's giving but, I believe we can't out give you."

It was shocking! It was nothing. Roosevelt and I wanted to see them. I cooked greens, spaghetti, and fried rice. I froze the spaghetti and greens and made snickerdoodle cookies the day before we left because my son loves it. I prepared the fried rice before we got on the plane. Why? I thought it would be nice to pull something out of the freezer made up and ready to go. I didn't have a reason except for love, I guess.

Lastly, understand that there is danger in giving. I have cut my kids off if I know they are ungrateful or don't value gifts or family. For example, I sent a calendar for the year with dates for Sunday dinner. I checked with my oldest to make sure he was available because he had a crazy sports schedule. Once a month, I had a Sunday dinner of about 12-15 people. It was for my boys, single women, and friends who did not have family in the city. I did this mainly for my boys so we could all be together. It was "First Sunday Dinner." No one had to cook or bring a dish. Just show up, eat, and take food home for the next couple of days.

The problem was that all my friends and their kids showed up, but the children I birthed grew too busy. I stopped First Sunday dinners immediately. The gift of time, a home-cooked meal, and fellowship were not significant. Six months went by without a drop of food. Then came February, the love month. I invited everyone for the First Sunday dinner, and I can honestly say that I did not have a problem getting them to attend. Building these kinds of experiences and lessons early is essential.

The same thing happened for my youngest son. He asked for some money. I told him it was not a gift, but it was only a loan. I asked him if he was positive he could pay it back and if he knew when. We were clear on the amount and the deadline for it to be returned. He didn't pay it back. He was cut off from receiving any more funds. His not honoring his word could lead to something more significant later in life. If I made excuses for him not paying me back or even gave him more money, it might have cost him his life.

Earlier, we shared about giving to the Lord first, saving, and then giving to ourselves. While practicing the love of giving, there are spiritual and physical rewards. You will find that you can't beat G-d's giving to you, and He will send what you need. Giving helps everyone have what they need! Practicing this lesson with your children while they are young will reduce their selfish tendency and help them be more willing to share themselves with you and others.

How do you teach this lesson?

Make a card, draw a picture, find something and give a penny or a nickel. Before the holiday, January, start a jar and drop all your extra coins in for Thanksgiving and Christmas. Make a plan on they can give to relatives on a special occasions.

Visit a senior citizen or grandparent and do something nice, read a book, watch a movie with them, make a dessert or bring dessert. Please talk about the benefit of giving and various ways to give. Discuss the friends in their environment that give and who they give to. Ask questions about the situations in which it occurs.

How will you see it in practice?

- Do they do for you or people around you?
- Do you see them give of their money and time?
- Do they discuss people or friends who take from them and others?

~~&~~ Notes from My Sons ~~&~~

GIVE more than you get! Give!

How much can you give? Because you cannot out-give God. It is better to give than receive.

— Corey

How to Give from My Heart

You are number one in the life lesson on how to give from the heart. Remember when we were at US Bank, and the teller had been struggling with her finances? You sent her some money, and she was so surprised. Or that time you brought Asha a car, and she wasn't even your blood. Or those times you tutored kids out of the kindness of your heart. It all shows how big your heart is. It offers the foundation of what you believe. I see it every day, every hour, every minute, every second. So I thank you for that lesson.

—Alan

It's always better to do more than less!

More is always better if possible. Sometimes you can only do what you can do. But, if there is an opportunity to do more, do it. I think this concept is a lost art. Most people do less when they should do more and miss out on the reward of more. I have had so many blessings in my life because I took the extra step on something small.

—Corey

How to Open My Heart

Opening your heart is a different lesson than giving from the heart. This lesson is about being vulnerable enough to let someone in, whether a friend, a lover, sister, or brother. What does it take to let someone in and give them all of yourself? You know how to do this. I've learned how you take a person in and breathe out love. Breathe in love and breathe out love. What a beautiful thing? I want to open my heart more than I can. You tend to accept more with an open heart. You give more with an open heart. You love more with an open heart. And I thank you for that lesson.

—Alan

Treat Javonne as God has treated you since you were born with love, honesty, and protection. Make her feel as if no one else in the world could even come close to how you treat her. Be her everything!

—Renny, Jr.

When Sydney was born, my mom told me to treat Sydney how I want her husband to treat her. Show her lots of love and do the small things, so she knows her daddy loves her. Like, write notes, give her lots of hugs and kisses, and tell her how beautiful and intelligent she is daily.

—Renny, Jr.

Mom would tell me, "While you're traveling with your basketball team across the country, your wife is sacrificing. Please make sure you do something nice for her before leaving and constantly bringing her something back home. Be A MAN!

—Renny, Jr.

Invest in People and Experiences

I honestly did not quite understand this lesson until I saw this idea in action with my very own eyes. I have seen my mother invest in people and love people her whole life. Now my mother has so many loved ones that adore her. So many people to call on and can potentially call on her. We are not built to live on an island; we were born to be together. We are considered the body of Christ.

Not only have people been a great love for my mom, but having incredible experiences with people has also been significant. What can we experience today? How can I maximize my life experiences? The only way to honestly do that is to spend time with people you enjoy being around and who enjoying being around you. I am so thankful for my friends and loved ones because they have been so committed to me for years. Thank you to all my loved ones!

—Corey

Life is a Gift so share It with the people that deserve it most! There is so little time in life. Although, it feels like life stretches this extended period. It does not. I learned so much from this life lesson. Watch who you hang with and where you invest your time because you may never get it back.

—Corey

"In everything give thanks; for this is the will of G-d in Christ Jesus concerning you."

— 1 Thessalonians 5:18

"Now on his way to Jerusalem, Jesus traveled along the border between Samaria and Galilee. (12) As He was going into a village, ten men who had leprosy met Him. ...(13) and called out in a loud voice, "Jesus, Master, have pity on us!" (14) ... And as they went, they were cleansed. (15) One of them, when he saw he was healed, came back, praising G-d in a loud voice. (16) He threw himself at Jesus' feet and thanked Him-and he was a Samaritan. (17) Jesus asked, "Were not all ten cleansed? Where are the other nine?"

— Luke 17:11-17

2

Gratitude

As a school principal and teacher, I was shocked by the number of adults who never said thank you. I would provide morning donuts, coffee, lunch, holiday treats. Rarely did you find all of the staff returning to say thank you to the giver. It appeared that the staff took kind gestures from others as deserved. I watched this as a teacher. It so left an impression on me to make sure my students would always be grateful. The ungrateful behavior caused me to prioritize the lesson of appreciation with students at school and my children at home. Practicing and writing thank you was a monumental lesson for my kids and students in my care to learn. Practice picking up the phone and calling (not texting), writing a note, and dropping it in the mailbox. When a person takes the time to write a note of gratitude, you feel something special about that person.

Gratitude is not just for gift giving, but for opening the door, putting food on the table, handing you something that you needed, teaching you something you didn't know, assisting a person from falling, doing hair, offering and providing a ride. When we demonstrate thankfulness, it says we took time to remember the giver's kindness and thoughtfulness. Gratitude reminds us that people care, and their resources and time should not be taken for granted. People don't have to care, do, or give. Help kids practice gratitude at an early age. Practice talking about why you write a note or say thank you. We are not entitled to the things we have or receive. They are gifts.

I did not teach another lesson, but I learned that life is a gift. Treat it with care. We live in an age where many people have access to firearms, and there are acts of violence on people's lives as if life has no meaning. The mere fact that we got woke up is a gift. As a mom, I didn't spend time teaching the importance of being careful with their life. Children should take a moment to recognize this gift because it can be gone in the blink of an eye. My kids have been in situations where they could have lost their lives. They are African-American men. One wrong word, being in the wrong place with the wrong group, or just walking down the street, and their lives could be over. Life is not a joke. Be grateful to G-d for your time and thankful to Him, who watches over the universe and you.

In one of the verses that introduced this lesson, Jesus healed nine lepers, and only one came back. Only one person knew the full extent of what Jesus did for them. Only one person valued the opportunity to return to their families, jobs, and freedom. Can you believe that the others did not think Jesus was worthy of a thank you? He healed all nine and changed them forever, but it wasn't worthy of a thank you. That verse showed us that if we are not careful, we could act in the same way. We could be so mesmerized by the gift that we forget about the giver. Be persistent in remembering that home is the practice run for the rest of your life. You are setting the stage for your family to be distinguished, not just okay. You want others to say, "Who is this amazing person?"

How do you teach this lesson?

Monitor how your child expresses thankfulness. Review notes that were written by your children. Ensure that they are publishable notes. Have your child read draft notes to you until they are ready for publishing. (Start reviewing all notes no matter what age.)

Have them practice how to write a note of gratitude. Your child is saying thank you in small and big things. Provide lovely notecards or colorful sheets of paper to write final revised notes and some stamps.

How will you see it in practice?

- Your child will not throw temper tantrums when they don't get something they want.
- Your child is embarrassed when they forget to be thankful/grateful.
- They express joy when receiving surprises, gifts, or favors (like having their favorite meal, snack, or going to their favorite restaurant). Your child doesn't expect things but shows gratefulness when they receive them.

~e~ **Notes from My Sons** ~e~

God says all you have to do is ask, and you shall receive according to his will. Instead of always asking God for what you need, be grateful for all your blessings by praying and thanking God for everything he has given to you!

—Renny, Jr.

Always say thank you right away with a phone call or a small note. It goes a long way.

—Renny, Jr.

Recognize the positive influences in your life because they can be quickly taken away.

—Renny, Jr.

"My commandment is this: Love each other as I have loved you."

—John 15:12

"We love because He first loved us."

—1 John 4:19

"For God so loved the world that He gave His one and only Son, that whoever believes in Him shall not perish but have eternal life."

—John 3:16

"And over all these virtues put on love, which binds them together in perfect unity."

—Colossians 3:14

"But God demonstrates His own love for us in this: While we were still sinners, Christ died for us."

—Romans 5:8

"And now these three remain: faith, hope, and love. But the greatest of these is love."

—1 Corinthians 13:13

3

Love

*L*OVE IS PROBLEMATIC BECAUSE IT requires that I think about and do for others. I put me last. In fact, I ensure that I am last. That is hard, but I believe that love never fails. Corey and I have many debates over this virtue. If love requires you to consider the other, then the two (family) in the relationship always think of the other person (members in the family). If I think about you and your needs and you think about me and my needs, it is always a win-win. When relationships fail, the other person is not the object of your love.

When children are little, it is all about them. During the holiday around our home, everyone is in "the hustle and bustle." One morning, while we were preparing to move and buy last-minute gifts, my granddaughter Harper sat in her chair, so snuggly, a big smile on her face, holding an iPad in one hand as her mom fed her. She did not have to lift a finger.

I said to her mom," That child is living the life."

Her mom was in a hurry, and she did not have time for Harper to play in her food, so she fed her. When a child lives a life such as that, they can't even begin to imagine that the world is not designed to make them happy. Children capture the undivided attention of parents, grandparents, older siblings, friends, etc., for 2-3 years. We are available all day, every day, to meet their needs. Then we start to teach some independence and want to let them fly, but the TERRIBLE 2s and 3s set incomplete with rebellion and tantrums because they want the old dependent life. They want a life where the entire world is about them.

The more we revolve the world around our kids, the harder it will be for them to see and understand someone else matters. Deciding to clamp down or implementing tough love may be so hard for some parents because all you wanted was that boy or girl, and now they are here. You can't get enough of their cute little faces and their adorable behavior. So you take pictures all the time. They are the center of your world, and you wait on them, ensuring that you will be there for them as soon as they call you. Then one day, reality comes, and you have to teach this lesson about love.

Kids want everything for themselves, so sometimes you have to demonstrate tough love. As much as I love my boys, each one has experienced the hand of tough love. When Renny Jr. had not saved any money and was living rent-free, he had to leave my home. When Corey decided that he wanted to live house to house, he had to go. When Alan wrecked his car, no other vehicle was provided for him. Each time I laid the hammer down, it was hard, but it was love, and it was for their good. They probably didn't like it, but they are all the better because of it.

Some of the experiences they were involved in did not make them (or me) proud. It caused great pain and terrible sadness. So much so that my soul felt burned and shattered. It caused me to feel like I didn't want to live to see the outcome. But, I had to implement tough love. I had to put some fences up, some rules of engagement, and brand-new expectations on how to live.

Feeling all the pain made me think that I didn't love them, but it wasn't that. It was this numbness from the pain. We might find ourselves doubting our love for our children and others when we encounter painful experiences. I have been there, as well as many of you. Sometimes the pain is so bad you have to throw in the towel or pull yourself together to think about love. I couldn't even pray about love, but I had to push past those feelings and still love. I had to work at loving. Our families will depend on it. As you recall from the previous lesson, sometimes we do not weigh our actions' cost, and the entire community is affected. After time passed and the Father above healed all my wounds, I wanted to share love again, and I wanted to love too.

Love is a strange phenomenon because you have to act against the grain of your being and the grain of society. Loving is not widespread. Look around. We have too many examples in our community, state, and nation of people hating and not loving. We have to create opportunities to love. When your children see you love, they replicate it. They do what you do.

It's important to note that love does not tolerate emotional, physical, and mental abuse. If you are experiencing this, run for help immediately. Love does not require you to stay in harmful situations and endure them. We must also practice this and teach our children how to count the cost of their actions and avoid hurtful or damaging encounters.

LOVE BREAKS DOWN YOUR GUARD. IT STOPS YOU FROM PUTTING UP A SHIELD.

When I led the Women's Ministry at my church, I desired for us to demonstrate love. I wanted us to be the first to step up and love, to be the most loving people anyone had ever encountered in church. I wanted us to be not only caring but lovable. I wanted us to see that winning new visitors' love would be a privilege and honor, not the other way around. Before small group ministries were famous, we created Red Tent Ministries. The purpose was to practice hospitality, love, and share in the word of G-d with the women in the church. In our groups, we practiced giving and loving, not how to do church or religion. We set the bar high to change our conduct and be women who loved. We had to demonstrate that we were not afraid to be the first person to love.

When I was a principal in the late 1980s, a person from the district office told me that the poor children (87% of the students were of lower socioeconomic status and primarily African American) would never achieve above the 50th percentile. I was so shocked. I just became a principal. I was trying all kinds of strategies to get my kids smart.

He said, "Sit back, kick your feet up! You are doing the best you can. Just keep them under control!"

He didn't say, "Linda, I know you are new to the role. I want to help you help your kids. Here are some strategies to ensure their success."

He said, "They will never achieve above the 50th percentile."

I couldn't accept that, and I didn't stop praying for a solution. I went to Houston, Texas, to watch the late Dr. Thaddeus Lott. He changed all kids' lives. If you were in his school, learning was the goal. Poor African-American, poor Latino, poor white kids achieved at the 98th percentile. On my return home, I cried all way! I begged G-d to help me change the lives of kids. G-d answered my prayer. I returned home and followed Dr. Lott's precise directions he implemented in Texas. It was that easy. Love says to find a way and do it. Love does what's best for others.

Before Jesus descended above, He gave one great commandment to "love one another, liked he loved". When we love and consider the needs of all children, then everyone wins. The world turns for the better. We have many intelligent kids around us who can replicate the meaning of love because someone loved them and sought out the best for them. Love is not far-reaching. Look and love.

Weekly, I watch Alan pick up roommates or take people who don't have transportation to the store or pick them up from work. I watch Corey make sure his nephew has what he needs to grow up the right way. Renny, Jr. gathers all of us (family and friends) to shop, prep, cook, and feed the homeless every December. Love requires you to look, see, and do. Talk to your kids about how to detect love. Love is different than a feeling. Feelings change by the situation or condition of the day. What does it look like when someone is looking out for your good? What does it look like when a person shows that they love you? What does it look like when you love first?

Share your love for your children with them and how you demonstrate it. Sometimes they don't know. Love looks different through the eyes of a kid. Talk to them about how you know they love you. Sometimes we can only do what we do until we can do better or different. Don't let social media be the parent of love or describe it to children. Get a jumpstart. Plant seeds of what you do to make their life more wonderful.

Spend the end of your evenings before bedtime sharing the examples of love you and your children have seen throughout the day. Examples of love could be things like making sure they are safe, praying for their well-being, being grateful that G-d answered your prayers at their birth, and sacrificing so they can have shelter, necessities, and some of their wants. Talk about how much fun they are to be around, their smile and genius, and how you like spending time with them as they grow up. Kids do a lot of talking, listening, and imitating in school. Intercede often with the best message for their life. Remember, home is the practice run for the rest of their life. Make it count.

How do you teach this lesson?

Present opportunities where your child can sacrifice small things for someone else. For example:

1. The last piece of bread at dinner time.
2. Sharing toys with friends.

Ask your child to assist you with things that are not standard requirements (chores/responsibilities).

How will you see it in practice?

- Your child will share a favorite toy.
- Your child willingly helps you with tasks outside of their chores.

~❧ **Notes from My Sons** ☙~

Love Never Fails!

If true love is included in everything, you will never fail. Love is all-encompassing that will supersede all things. For God so loved the world that he gave his only begotten son! I am so thankful for lessons of love. If you had a failed relationship, it's most likely due to a lack of love. Because love never fails!

—Corey

Huge life lesson for me! Love conquers all things!!!!!

—Corey

"I am trying to become a lover and understand what it means to use the word love. When talking about love, I can quote only the greatest lover I know: Dr. Linda L. Gibson, who would say, "I love nothing more than giving and caring about giving."—not giving in the sense of material wealth but the giving of time, giving inspiration and giving feelings. Not caring about giving in the sense of I want to give to you because you gave to me, but I want to give to a person because I want to show them how I feel, that I love them, that their happiness is important to me. Too often in this world, do we emphasize giving to receive and love to be loved. That is why every time I catch you giving (I see it all the time, you cannot even tell when you are giving, it is a part of who you are, it is your personality). I say it has to be G-d. It is G-d because only G-d speaks to unconditional love no matter what, and that is what you show all of the time. I am working every day to be more of a lover because the world is so harsh, and we have to live in it every day. I love you because you gave me the blueprint, and I just got to build it. "U feel me." And Keep I have to keep G-d in it, and I can never fail."

—Corey

You show me how to love. Again, you tell me what love is; you show me why true love always stands the test of time. I hope you understand how love radiates off of you. It glows masterfully and with decadence. But every person you are around, you show love. From the handshake to the hug to just a smile. From the bank teller to the employee at MacDonald's. You show love. To your male friend, you cooked dinner, had a glass of wine, and laughed with by the fireplace. That's love. That's how you show someone you care for that you love them. It's always the little things I've watched you do. So, thank you for that lesson.

—Alan

First and foremost, thank you for letting me go. I know it must have been so hard, a struggle between your will and G-d's. But honestly, it has been the best thing that has ever happened. So thank you for your bravery, your courage but most of all, your faith. Thank you for taking a chance to create boundaries, praying, and giving me your ever-lasting love. ... Your support during my discovery has been so special and such an accurate picture of G-d's love for us all. Unconditional love will never be able to separate your love for your children. I can't thank you enough for all you do, but to show you through actions. I love you and wish only the best for the most beautiful mom I'll ever know.

—Alan

"Greater love has no one than this, that he lay down his life for his friends."

—JOHN 15:13

"I no longer call you servants because a servant does not know his master's business. Instead, I have called you friends for everything that I have learned from My father I have made known to you.

—JOHN 15:15

"Two are better than one because they have a good return for their work: (10) If one falls down, his friend can help him up. But pity the man who falls and has no one to help him up! (11) Also, if two lie down together, they will keep warm. But how can one keep warm alone? (12) Though one may be overpowered, two can defend themselves. A cord of three strands is not quickly broken."

—ECCLESIASTES 4:9-12

4

LIFE LESSON NO.

Family and Friends

I LOVE MY FAMILY AND FRIENDS. Fortunately, I have a great group of friends who are like my sisters. One reason for this particular lesson is accountability. I have seen marriages destroyed and children lost for years because there is no accountability for correction or direction. So, they are left to their selfish destruction. When you have family and friends who love you, they want you to know the truth, even when it hurts. Your greatness is their desire. It is not possible to be great on your own.

During my first year of marriage with Roosevelt, I went on a girlfriend trip to Washington DC. I left my husband with one chore to do. "When the lady comes to get the piano, open the door. Don't forget we are painting the house. The piano is in the way."

He said, "No problem!"

When the movers came to get the piano, he didn't answer the door. He was in the basement fast asleep. As the story goes, the lady called me to say the movers were at the door. No one would let them in, and they had to go.

I screamed, "No! Please don't leave."

Finally, I reached my husband. On the inside, I was, crying, screaming, and yelling, but not at him. I didn't talk to him. He apologized, but the piano was still at the front door. I started yelling at my girlfriends, telling them how he only had one chore. Not two. Just one. My friends let me vent for nearly two hours before telling me to stop. Darcel and Cynthia shared that my husband made a mistake, and he didn't mean it.

Then Cynthia said, "And he will make more."

Cynthia came into the house on our return home to check on Roosevelt, asking if he wanted her to stay until the next day to make sure he would be okay. It was so loving! That day made him aware of the love my girlfriends not only had for me but him, and, in return, it caused Roosevelt to love Cynthia and Darcel even more. He knew he was in hot water. He knew that once those ladies walked out that door, he might be buried in the back yard. But I couldn't get out the shovels because they talked me off the ledge. They talked sense in me.

Everyone was trying to find a truck, a mover, someone to get that piano out of the front hall. Roosevelt was full of remorse. I watched how bad he felt for disappointing me. Roosevelt felt more pain than me because he knew if I asked for something, I needed it. He didn't make an excuse for his behavior. He said," It should have never happened! I should have done that one thing for you."

When you are in a family of people who know what's right, even when it is your homegirls, it is their responsibility to speak up for what is right. When you do what is right, everyone wins! During the week following my husband missing the movers, he was at a stoplight, and a truck went by that said, "Piano Movers. Call us." He immediately wrote the number down. He gave me the number, and I called to provide them with the piano's make and model. The movers came to test the piano and bought it for four times more than the first buyers. When you do right, and your heart is right, right things happen for you.

Roosevelt could have acted crazy. He could have said, "So what? Stay home next time."

I could have gone crazy, minimized, and degraded him, but I didn't, and he didn't. When we treat each other like the family we love, the Lord gives us more than we could ever imagine.

Sometimes family members want to hold secrets, they are too ashamed by the hurt, or sometimes, I can admit, it is too much to bear. Sometimes you don't know how to say or deal with the hard stuff. I encourage you to try. I encourage you to cultivate a culture in your family of honesty without penalty. Have a family meeting time. I wish I had been able to do more of this with my boys. When you are in separate households, it isn't easy.

Be encouraged to work on building a culture of trust and support. It is hard because we want our children to get what we expect right, so our meetings can become all about what they did wrong, not what they need to get it right. Sad to say, it happens like that for our spouses too. If you find that your family meetings have become that, change. Try to have a counseling period following an inappropriate or incorrect action. If a family meeting is about a "good-beat-down," it will not be productive. Remember, you are the coach, and if the team is not effective, then the coach must try a different strategy or make time for additional practices.

Come together twice a month to check in. At the end of each week, Roosevelt and I have a review of the past week. What went well? What happened? Any improvements needed? Do we need any adjustments in the upcoming week? I held teachable moments with my kids when something popped up, when they didn't understand something, or were going left. I kept the goal-setting meeting to review ways for all of us to change or improve.

It is essential to teach children the value of having someone love them enough to want the best for them. Home is the place to run and fall. Parents have a good idea about the discipline necessary to improve behavior when their children fail. We spend time in the early years disciplining to prevent an uncaring society from tampering with our kids' lives. When people don't know you or care about you, they will apply the same punishment or consequence to your children they give to all kids. They don't care how you raised them. Do everything you can to prevent the outside world from negatively impacting your kids. The prison system works hard to get our kids and keep them. It is a billion-dollar business, which is the reason there is so much practice is needed at home to prevent our children from entering a system designed to take their independence and livelihood from them.

There is no escape from the road of life and what lies ahead. There is no stopping the challenges that may unexpectedly roll out of nowhere, but we can prepare our kids with the right tools to strategically design, plan, and excavate through the hard stone and debris. The family works through experiences and situations to demonstrate how you overcome obstacles and strategies to create the best solutions and who should or can be involved. I wish I had perfected this lesson in my family. Model the steps your child needs to consider in a difficult situation. Do not give them all the answers but show them how to eliminate the wrong or harmful decisions.

Please don't close your eyes and say your family and friends aren't your business. Don't let train wrecks come and stay silent. Trains are used for transportation, but they can kill you. When you see a train approaching, do something! Everyone is connected to someone. All choices impact your connections. There is no way around it. Whatever happens for my children, good or bad, I feel joy and pain. If someone hurts them or they hurt someone, I feel the pain. My children are older. Teaching lessons early and consistently will hopefully minimize the feeling of pain so you and your children can enjoy more joyful experiences. The more you teach and coach, the more experiences and lessons your children can have to ensure positive choices.

Finally, it is essential to remember the benefits of being in the Family of G-d. Pastor Robert often reminds us that we are in the family of a loving Father who seeks to be with us through every valley and mountain we climb. He knows the future, and He knows exactly what we need to be our best and to give Him Glory.

How do you teach this lesson?

Introduce opportunities to connect with family and friends. Lead by example by calling family members/friends. Be mindful of your child (offering assistance or providing unexpected gifts or favors).

How will you see it in practice?

- Your child will duplicate or mirror the actions you have shown.

~ Notes from My Sons ~

I've always had trouble doing this from day one, and I still do, but it gets better every day. You've asked, "How do you feel?" or "What's going on?" or you would say, "Talk to me." I remember the day we were sitting around the dinner table at 868 Franklin, and for some reason, I just started crying, and I don't know why. You got me up from the table, and you took me to the couch, and you held me, and you started crying as well, with me. You said, "I can't help you if you don't tell me what's wrong." and I asked, "Why are you crying?" and you replied with tears running down your eyes, "Because when you are hurting, I am hurting." That was when feelings became so apparent, and I started to pluck at them bit by bit. So thank you for that lesson.

—Alan

Throughout the years, you have been open and honest about others that have come and gone throughout our households. From past husbands and other girlfriends who have come and gone from our home, you have taught me how to see who truly loves you and who indeed doesn't. You always gave me just enough information to make sure I knew who to trust and who not to trust. Have I taken that information with me everywhere? Maybe not, as I often put my faith and trust in a lot of people. But I thank you for those little tidbits of information. And I thank you for that lesson.

—Alan

Keep Your Family Close and your Brothers even closer!
The family is everything to me. It is my fuel and my passion. I want to succeed at a higher level to be an immense blessing to my family. The crazy thing is that you don't pick your family, but I could never see myself without them in my life.

—Corey

As the oldest brother, mom always told me to look out for your brothers at all cost. I lived my life to be an excellent example for my brothers; on how to execute themselves properly in the classroom, sports, the community, and how to treat family and friends. That came from my mom; thank you!

—Renny, Jr.

5

Respect Everyone

"Show proper respect to everyone: Love the brother-hood of believers, fear God honor the King."

—1 Peter 2:17

URING MY FIRST FULL YEAR teaching in a city school district, a student drew a truck running me over. I posted the picture on the bulletin board with the rest of his classmates' work. At Open House, a formal opportunity to meet your child's teacher, my third-grade student's parents showed up. I asked him to talk about his drawing to his parents. His mother was outraged. He was shocked that his picture was on display with the rest of his classmates. He described why he decided on the drawing and wanted everyone to know. He didn't share with me, but he did share with his parents. He reminded me of that incident and how it left an impression in his mind on how his parents reacted, and I didn't.

No matter how big or small, I respect all people, no matter their color, gender, or position. Everyone deserves respect. That third-grader is my friend today. He maintained contact with me, and I showed up at his high school events and birthday celebrations. His daughter played with my godchildren. I never let his biases about people tarnish my respect for him as a boy learning in school, who he was, and what kind of person I was.

Children need to know how to be respectful. I worked with some very unruly, disrespectful, and careless adults. As a principal, I have been called a "B" and "MF." You name it. But I never lost my composure. I never allowed their disrespect to ignite my anger toward them. I focused on a solution to the problem. Respect means I will listen and respond. I don't have to be your friend, I don't have to hang out with you, but I can speak and say good morning and acknowledge that I see you.

Respect has to be the hardest lesson to teach because you are the model. The way you talk to and treat your kids, neighbors, people you work with, and how you talk on the phone demonstrates how you respect people. Consider how you conduct yourself at the grocery store, restaurant, and mall when things are not what you expected. It is hard to tell kids to respect someone when they might hear and see the opposite. Our body language, tone, and the types of words we use provide a good idea of how we feel about a person. Every day we model how to respect each other. You and I model how to do right or wrong. We will do this every day for the rest of our lives. Our kids are always watching. That is a great weight on our shoulders.

Alan wrote in his note that the lesson he learned was sneaking candy into the movies. Do you think I wanted him to learn that lesson? No. Did that benefit me at that time? Yes! But look at the message that I sent, that stealing from the theater was okay. It is not okay. When I read that, I felt horrible. I didn't want that to be my message. Kids work in the movie theatre. If everyone brought candy in and didn't buy it at the concession stand, someone could lose a job. That is disrespectful to an establishment. When I read his note, I couldn't believe he remembered those movie experiences after all these years, yet there it was, upfront and center in my face. He taught me that kids watch everything. Now, Alan is a young man, think about how long ago he got an unintentional lesson?

How do you teach this lesson?

Teach your child the Golden Rule (treat others the way you want to be treated). Present your child with opportunities to express when others' behaviors are not respectful.

Note: You may not be able to control your or your child's environment fully but guard their environment as much as possible and check in with your child as much as possible to reaffirm proper behavior (for them and others).

How will you see it in practice?

1. Your child will not use derogatory words or engage in name-calling.
2. Your child will be able to identify inappropriate behavior.

✎ Notes from My Sons ✎

I still remember like it was yesterday when we drove to the AMC, and you brought candy and pop beforehand, and I was so appalled at the idea of you, my angel of a mother, sneaking these items into the movie theater. Welp! Now I understand and do the same thing. So, thank you for that lesson.

—Alan

Make sure to respect your elders and those individuals that have come before you in life!

I have learned that all you have to do is watch others see where their lives have ended up and get a perfect idea of where your life may end up making similar decisions. Watching my elders has given me a powerful guide around what not to do or what to do in life. I genuinely respect my elders! I am thankful to know individuals that have lived long and productive lives.

—Corey

It seems that these days our elders are not that respected by younger people. Maybe with the internet and the wealth of knowledge available to the world, we no longer think we need personal guidance in life. I beg [to] differ! I think it is more important to cling close to elders to understand their journey and story better. The elders in my life have so blessed me, and I will continually respect every one of them.

I can remember when I was in high school, and my mom would say, "I'm your head coach, so be respectful to your paid coach who stands up and leads the team, but remember I will lead you far better!"

—Renny, Jr.

How to Treat Women with Respect
From day one, you had us opening doors for women, lifting heavy things for women, and walking on the women's left side. You ingrained in my head, a man respects woman, period, and I admire that. Although some women nowadays don't like it, I have always been acknowledged by others for the kindness and respect you instilled in me. So, I thank you for that lesson.

—Alan

Do onto others as you would want them to do unto you!
Interesting life lesson for the modern person/believer. This lesson is interesting because you no longer have to treat people like you want to be treated with social media and other less formal communication modes. It would be easy to hide behind the social media platform, screen names, nicknames, false profiles, etc. I think it is more critical today than ever before to treat people the right way.

I remember when I first learned this lesson. I had to be in middle school, maybe in the 6th grade. My mother and I were riding in the car. Mom focused on getting me to the next place safely, and I was in the passenger seat looking out the window making funny faces, throwing up crazy signs, and teasing drivers as they passed our car. I was having so much fun. Then my mother finally caught on to what I was doing, and she immediately put a halt to the fun in the car.

Like most moms, she wanted to know what she was doing and why? My answer was I don't know and nothing. My mother then explained why it's essential for me not to play with people but to treat them how I wanted to be treated. Because one day, I will be the person on the other end. How would I feel if the same things I was doing to others also happened to me?

This life lesson was a crucial part of my growth from a child to a young adult. If I treated people with a lack of care and respect, wouldn't it make sense that someday a person would treat me the same way? It dawned on me that it was better to treat everyone initially how I wanted to be treated. Or at the very least, treat people with a minimal level of respect. From that point in the car until now, I have tried to treat all people with a minimal level of care, and more often than not, I have tried to treat everyone like I wanted to be treated.

—Corey

Give your best every day in everything!

I learned this lesson very early in life. I remember my first- or second-time playing basketball for a recreation center. I was part of a team at Schiller Rec. At that time, I was the best person on the team. Because I was the best on the team, I felt as if I could slack off during the winning games. The game I decided to slack off was the game that my entire family came to see. I was playing around, and I had an audience of family members that I truly wanted to impress at that moment.

I lost a valuable moment to show my family what I could do on the Basketball court. I was so angry, and I remember after the game my mom saying, "Do you wish you would have played more seriously?" I said "yes." Then my mom said, "That's why you always give it your best no matter who is watching because you never know who will be watching."

From that day on, I always tried to give my very best in every area of my life. Today I get upset with myself if I feel like I could have done better than the outcome I achieved.

Give it all you got!!!

—Corey

I can remember my first year at Hampton, and I played around being a C student, knowing I could execute at a higher level. I came home over Christmas break and sat down with mom, and we talked about my grades. I remember this like it was yesterday, and she said, "I'm paying for four years of college, and then you're on your own." It's crazy how God wakes you up with words because I had been hearing stories about students taking 5 and 6 years to graduate. I went back to school and hit the books firm, and now I finished my second master's degree.

—Renny, Jr.

Get your work done Immediately!
Please do what you have to do and do it now! I learned now is better than later. Why wait? Tomorrow is not promised. Why would I wait for anything? Who are you waiting for? It's been one of my calling cards in life. "Corey Tyson does not wait. He gets stuff done immediately." I learned that the more I do now, the less I will need to do later.

—Corey

Every Christmas, it worked. Every birthday, it triumphed. You, money, and tissue paper are never the right combinations because you always have some trick up your sleeve with both. But every time we would put our hands in a box or shake the gifts the night before, we would never know. You know the element of surprise. Thank you for teaching me how to orchestrate surprises. So thank you for teaching that lesson.

—Alan

When you leave the house, look your very best!
More now than ever, people judge you before they even get to know you. We could also say put your best foot forward every day. Not only do we put our best foot forward, but we know how to act. First impressions are pivotal to your success when dealing with people.

—Corey

6

Balance

"There is a time for everything, and a season for every activity under heaven: (2) a time to be born and a time to die, (4) a time to weep and a time to laugh, a time to mourn and a time to dance, (5) a time to scatter stones and a time to gather them, a time to embrace and a time to refrain, (6) a time to search and a time to give up, a time to keep and a time to throw away (7) a time to tear and a time to mend, time to be silent and a time to speak, (8) a time to love and a time to hate, a time for war and a time for peace."

—Ecclesiastes 3:1-9

I JUST FINISHED MY CHILDREN'S BOOK *GET Smart*. It is a small book inspired by my grandbaby Harper. Alan asked me how I felt about completing my first book. I said,

"Okay," because I was waiting for this book or for *Doc's House* to be completed. These were bigger, and I had been working hard to get them.

He said, "Mom! You better stop and fall on your knees and thank G-d for what you have done!"

I said, "Well, Okay!"

He said, "Mom, you have to stop and be in the moment and enjoy it! Don't let it slip by."

He was right. I was so busy trying to meet deadlines, monitor the illustrators, get ready for Thanksgiving and Christmas that I didn't even breathe or fall on my knees to be thankful. I minimized the accomplishment. It didn't seem big enough!

There is something exceptional about taking time to rest, to smell all the flowers, even the dandelions! I failed to do that, and Alan reminded me of the importance of every step we take, to stop and genuinely enjoy the steps you took to reach a goal, help someone, or enjoy a gift you received. Stop looking for the next moment or the next thing because it is not guaranteed. I know life is a gift. Alan reminded me to do that.

As a mom and a single parent, you can get busy being busy, and never stop to smell the roses, especially when kids are in middle and high school.

"Auntie, I can't wait until I grow up so I can go on trips and travel," my niece Michelle once said to me.

I said, "You can do that now."

She was amazed. All trips aren't expensive. You can take a three-day cruise for $300.00 per person. You may not have a balcony cabin, but your destination will not be any different. You can go to a city and stay in a hotel. Swim, walk the city, attend the free events. Every city has them. Does it take time and effort to find those deals? Absolutely, but you can do it.

We had Family Day on Sunday when my boys were young. It was generally a bowling activity or playing basketball at the gym. We would go to the movies, ride around in the car, or get a scoop of ice cream. We stopped and spent time together. With my husband, Roosevelt, I take him on Saturday adventures. We grab a breakfast sandwich, a drink and start driving. Sometimes I know where we are going. Other times I don't. Sometimes we drop coffee and donuts at a friend's house. We chat from the car and keep it moving. We just spend time together. Why? You can work yourself to death, and tomorrow may not come.

I cannot emphasize it enough. There are no promises for tomorrow, and if tomorrow comes, you have no idea the condition of your health or the country. During the year 2020, so many people planned trips (myself included) that were all canceled. The entire nation had to stay home. When you think about putting things off, don't. Enjoy your life at the capacity available to you.

Work and no play impact our relationships and our health. Work hard and play. There is something very restful about enjoying the flowers, enjoying the smell of coffee, and looking at the ones you love. During this season, I have enjoyed this time at home. I made the most of it. I worked diligently, but I made sure to rest even in an unrestful, intensive situation.

It is essential to take time to breathe and know that it is okay!

How do you teach this lesson?

Put time for rest and family time on your calendar. Call older kids up and have them come over for dessert or breakfast. Play games.

How will you see it in practice?

- Have kids take turns planning events for the family.
- Kids inquire about activities to help family members come together.
- Kids want to ask for alone time.

✸ Notes from My Sons ✸

Laugh, enjoy life, enjoy where you are in life and don't take yourself so seriously. But most of all, be happy!

Life is too short to be worried and upset. I have so often failed at this life lesson probably because I have it listed at number 7 on my life lessons list.

Although, as of today, I have turned over a new leaf. I am ready to smile and have fun. I am no longer going to be 100% work. I am enjoying every bit of life, even when I am at work. Now is the time to win and enjoy life. Not later! Keep smiling, and everything will work out in the end!

—Corey

"Let another praise you, and not your own mouth; someone else, and not your own lips."

—Proverbs 27:2

"As iron sharpens iron, so one man sharpens another."

—Proverbs 27:17

"Charm is deceptive, beauty is fleeting, but a woman who fears the Lord is to be praised."

—Proverbs 31:30

7

Praise

*A*S A PRINCIPAL AND AN observer of teacher instructional practices, I calculated the number of times a teacher gave students specific praise statements in five minutes. Generally, they made one or two praises or none at all. I felt terrible for the kids. I thought about how kids were rarely praised at school or home.

Your specific praise gives life to a child. I work at how I give a compliment. I try to spell out what my kids, husband, or friends do to please me. I work not to give general compliments like "good job." I try to make sure that students know I am aware of how they are smart, what made their job good, how they were generous, and what kind of action they displayed that made me proud. I say words like, "I love the way you remembered to put the trash out, and I didn't have to ask you, " "I love the way you thought about my favorite candy and bought it for me," or "I love how you helped your friend when they needed someone."

We naturally give directions and make corrections, but rarely do we honestly look at how someone behaves and praise it. It is not natural. It takes practice. Specific praise is like honey. The person starts thinking of their positive characteristics and attributes. They start seeing themselves in a more positive light. Inappropriate behavior can be turned around by finding the specific good in them. I loved an old movie called *Polyanna*. She came into a city where no one saw anything good in anybody. She looked for every person's specific good, which caused the change in the city's direction. Can you imagine that your words can change your child's life? Your comments can help them think of only the good in them.

Specific praise will melt the hearts of men and women, boys and girls. I know you will not believe me. Try an experiment. Have someone in your family count how many times you praise each other. Turn on the timer and count for 15-20 minutes. Write down the specific praise that is provided to anyone in your family. This lesson is critical because the old statement that "sticks and stones may break my bones, but words will never hurt me" is a lie. Words can kill you. So, the more we lift each other with expressions that align with value and respect, the better you and your kids will feel.

How do you teach this lesson?
Start by providing specific praises on the things that they do.

How will you see it in practice?
They should start specific praises to you and each other.

❧ Note from My Sons ❧

Praise came every day in the household. Praise for thought or doing some minor household tasks. Recognition went for all three of us, and we would all know it. There would be a jubilant dance with hands in the air and a loud cry praising the Lord and praising us. This seemed to be a critical addition to anything one of us would do. Although at the time, and still sometimes today, it looks over the top, children and even your adults need this. I've seen too many kids with no self-esteem or no confidence in what they do. Praise gives that confidence in what they do and will do and the confidence to keep going no matter what lies ahead. Praise provides us with the assurance we are on the right path.

—Alan

"Many are the plans in a man's heart but, it is the Lord's purpose that prevails."

—PROVERBS 19:21

"The purpose of a man's heart are deep waters, but a man understanding draws them out."

—PROVERBS 20:5

8

LIFE LESSON NO.

Seek to Find
their Talents

PENDING TIME OBSERVING AND PAYING attention to what people like, what they seem to be good at, unique gifts, and talents is a skill I acquired over time. I am intentional about listening and inquiring about people's choices and desires. Corey watched TV at eight or nine years of age on buying properties and houses. One day he and his friend Sheena set up a yard sale. The most peculiar discovery about this yard sale was Sheena and Corey knocked on the neighbors' doors, asking them to come to their yard sale. I knew to keep my eye on these characteristics because he was probably going to be in sales. During the season of trying to find himself, he graduated from college and was working in sales. He decided he wanted to go to law school and pursue a Master of Business Administration (MBA). I begged him not to do it.

I said, "Please don't do it! Sure, get an MBA, but not a law degree."

He was positive that it was something he wanted. I told him it did not fit what he liked to do. He went to law school, stayed a year and a half, and $100,000 later, said it was not what he thought it would be. All of his life, he has been selling something, and today he is still selling.

Understanding your gifts and talents is so important. When I ask people how they choose their field of study, they report it is the only thing they ever wanted to do. I am so excited for them. They found the love for something early and didn't stop until they made it happen. Expose your children to as many opportunities as possible. If I had an inkling that writing briefs and researching were Corey's gift or interest, I would have put him in the environments to observe how lawyers prepare and research to attend court, design briefs, and meet clients.

Early on, Alan produced puppet shows, crafted buildings, and put together three-dimensional structures. He drew and created stage sets. Alan starred in commercials at the age of eight years old. He never stopped and never veered. Additionally, he has an administrative and organizational talent which allows him to organize events, direct and produce shows, and write. But his first love is acting. I can still picture Renny Jr. at the age of four sitting beside his dad, totally engaged in football and basketball. He has played sports since age 3 ½ and now works in the area of sports.

When I saw an area of interest, I immediately started feeding it. I built my children's capacity in the area they were most passionate about participating in.

When Renny, Jr. went to college, I said, "Get a degree in education. Major in physical education."

Did he listen? No. He wanted a degree in sports management. Based on his interest in athletics, I thought long-term. If he received a degree in physical education, he could teach, coach, and eventually become an Athletic Director. He didn't believe or truly trust my advice. Now, he has 3 degrees: a Master's in Sports Leadership, a Master's in Business Administration (MBA), a focus in Health Administration and Organizational Leadership, and a Bachelor of Science in Sports Management. But what would he love to do? Be an athletic director or coach. So what does he do as a part-time job? He runs his own Non-Profit for boys and girls in basketball, and he trains kids on the fundamental skills of basketball. He organizes basketball events for adults, boys, and girls in 5th grade and beyond. Who helps and is out there selling and cooking hot dogs and working the concession? My husband, his brother, wife, daughter, and me. All hands and feet are on board, still helping with his dream.

As a principal, I looked for talents in my teachers, and I directed them, massaged it, and gave them leadership opportunities. When people find their gift and talent, everyone benefits. If you are good at doing hair, constructing buildings or structures, organizing (things, places, people, etc.), singing, dancing, coding, plumbing, or cars, the earth and people around you benefit from your expertise. We need people who are excellent around us in the field they love. The whole community wins, we get excellent service, and you get paid the value of your worth. The more the right people get in the right place, the more pleasant and productive the world will be.

Earlier in my career, a lady told me the problem with education was that so many women hated their work in the field. They never wanted to be teachers, but the only positions they could choose from were a secretary, nurse, or teacher. So whenever that group of women retired, schooling would be better for kids and adults. I know you and I have worked with people who hate their jobs but depend on the check. Do you see why helping the people in our community find and use their passion is important?

This year my granddaughter Harper inspired me to write several children's books, but my book *Get Smart* was specifically for her. I wanted her to know that she is in charge of her destiny. Being born at 24 weeks of gestation meant that she could be limited physically, mentally, and even socially. But she is not! She had to overcome so many obstacles. There were things she could not do on her own, simple things like breathing, lifting her head, rolling over, or sitting up (something we take for granted). I watched her daily in the hospital trying to make a go at life, and she did. She is still tiny, but she is mighty! When I spend time with her, I am amazed by her confidence, fearlessness, and laser focus on anything she pursues. We call her unstoppable!

How do you teach this lesson?
Keep your eyes open. Watch what they do and say. Make connections.

How will you see it in practice?
They will do more things they love to do.

～ **Notes from My Sons** ～

I've always wondered why men don't know how to cook. It is truly the window to the soul. When someone cooks for me, I melt. When I cook for someone, they melt. I value our time in the kitchen. I appreciate our time to connect over making rolls from scratch. I love the way to make sure the mac n' cheese isn't too milky but oh so cheesy. I value just being in the kitchen because, in that place, it was only me, and you were talking and laughing and growing. I still treasure it, even though it's only me. I find the delicious recipes and then show you pictures of my creation as I learn the art of cooking again. I thank you for that lesson.

—Alan

Mom gave me space to grow up and make my mistakes to become a man. She never forced anything upon me other than being the best student at all times.

—Renny Jr.

Mom always told me that I should play soccer, basketball, and baseball once I entered high school. But thinking I knew what I wanted, I only played basketball. To this day, I should have listened.

—Renny Jr.

How to be Calm

Being calm may be the biggest thing that people hate and love about me. They don't understand how I can be so quiet in every single situation. When life calls for this dramatic response or when life wants me to seem like it's an emergency, I can't. I can't be dramatic about a specific situation because I know, by watching you, that God will make it okay. And knowing this, I don't overreact or rush because God has his plan laid out no matter what. Quiet or calm could still be a good or bad thing, but I appreciate it. Thank you for that lesson.

—Alan

Challenge

"Now to Him who is able to do immeasurably more than all we ask or imagine according to his power that is at work within us (21) to Him be glory in the church and in Christ Jesus throughout generations, forever and ever! Amen."

—Ephesians 3:20

DON'T FORGET THAT LEARNING TO MASTER ALL THESE SKILLS MAKES YOUR LOVED ONES INDEPENDENT OF THE TEACHER AND HELPS THEM BECOME THE TEACHER.

Home and school are the practice run for the rest of your life. Practicing being the best enables so many others to be helped or transformed. Our life is not our own. Our Father in heaven paid a high price for our lives. Our life matters to G-d. Our lives touch so many others, so the more we do to become all we can, the more it will help the people we touch.

Teaching in your home will directly impact another family, the community, and the world. Being distinguished sets the bar high but also says it is attainable. You have the power to change the trajectory of a person who does not know that being more is possible with practice. But you will be able to tell a story more extraordinary than mine. Your family will write how they practiced and got better. You will tell the story of losing hope and finding it. The most enjoyable part is you spent five minutes a day practicing and making it happen. The challenges got more comfortable, your love for one another grew more in-depth, and then your kids started teaching you.

I am so grateful you picked up this book today, and you got to the end. I encourage you to digest lessons, think about my sons' voices, and make a plan on where you will begin. Choose one or two life lessons or soft skills that you will implement for five minutes each.

Create your indicators of success and discover what success will look like to you. Everyone will benefit from the time you spend creating the best person inside.

While putting food on the table, clothes on children's backs, and being involved in activities are essential, be diligent in teaching everlasting values to sustain a person all the days of their lives. Help our children develop a vision for their future and a way to get there. Don't leave their success to chance. Set high expectations for living in a world that may not provide the steps to success or show them the road they will embark upon.

Remind your kids that obstacles, curves, pitfalls, potholes, unexpected and unforeseen circumstances, challenges, and celebrations are expected on their journey, so sit tight and ride it to the end. Prepare them over the many years in your care with the knowledge of what lies ahead so that they won't be fearful or afraid but confident that they are built to conquer and be successful. They are not only equipped for success, but they belong to the Family of G-d. His arms are open, and He remains ready to be on their journey. All they have to do is ask.

As a parent, family member, or friend, you are there to be the rope they can hold on to. You are there to be a secure lifeline as they take small leaps of faith each day. Tug on the rope when you see them headed for trouble. Remind them to use what they have learned in their practice sessions. Show and tell them that they are not alone, that if they see the danger, they can ask for help. Remind your children to never be afraid to reach back and look up! There is always a lifeline. Your children have you and they are never without the Father.

Lastly, let your children know they have practiced, they are prepared, and the world is waiting for them.

Part IV

Testimonies

If you're still contemplating if you should teach these lessons, read these testimonies, accounts of the final thoughts from my sons and letters lifted from connections and experiences I've had with loved ones over the years.

✑ Final Thoughts from My Sons ✑

Mom, thank you for your life lessons! There are plenty more, but I could only write 20 because we will be here all night otherwise. I don't know where I would be without them. Your commitment to developing your children has been incredible, and you're still not done. As our family and friends listen to our book of lessons, know that it has been a process that had started 60 years ago when you were born June 20, 1957. I love you, and thank you for being my rock, spiritual leader, and coach.

—Renny, Jr.

Wow, how do I begin this story? What do I say? How do I put my feelings on paper? Allow me to start with a portion of a short poem:

"When things go wrong as they sometimes will.

When the road you're trudging seems all uphill.

When funds are low and debts are high.

And you want to smile, but you have to sigh.

… Life is queer with its twists and turns.

As every one of us sometimes learns.

And many failures turn about.

When he may have won had he stuck it out: don't give up though the pace seems slow-you may succeed with another blow.

Success is failure turned inside out-

The silver tint of the clouds of doubt, and you never can tell how close you are.

It may be near when it seems so far: So, stick to the fight when you're hardest hit— it's when things seem worst that you must not quit."

Mom, this poem captures your life with me for my 26 years of experience. Your strength is an amazing inspiration to my daily living. I will go as far as to say it's fuel to my physical engine. I think about how G-d has blessed me with such a loving and caring mother who has never given up on life, love, and her Lord. Through your examples, I am blessed by my current circumstance. But I often feel uncomfortable or, more plainly stated, I'm not done yet. I am so ready for more clarity, consistency, and courage toward G-d's eternal plan for my life.

There is a level of excellence I wish to experience. There is a knowledge that I have not learned. I feel there is a new perspective hiding over the next horizon as I continue to press forward. I will get to that place where G-d can use me. I want to change, grow, and have absolute freedom, Mother. I need more prosperity for our families. (It seems like I want so much!)

Mom, I'm so thankful for you. My love for you is sincere, and it will continue until I have no more breath. So, I will press forward, proving to the world that I can deal with the conflict; I am more than a conqueror. Thank you, and I love you.

—Corey

I don't know what the future holds. I wish I could understand. And I wish I could go back, not grow up so fast, and stay at home a little longer. I wish I had more time. But enough wishing I could or had. I must stay present and be with myself now. Because the more I look back, the darker the future appears. Again, in between a rock and a hard place, I thank you for joining me on this journey and keeping me close to you. Thank you for teaching me so much, giving me so much, and loving me so much, no matter how hardheaded I became. I value you. I appreciate your teachings. I value your heart. I value your strength. I value your faith. But most of all, I value your endless love. And I can't get enough!

—Alan

Letters Lifted

Stacie Daniels (My 5th-grade student who is a lawyer, accountant, writer, and author)

Someday, I would love to be a teacher. It is a dream I have to educate my people, who are often left to fend for themselves in the lion's den of today's school systems. Too often, our people are not given the attention, direction, and knowledge needed to survive in this dog-eat-dog world. We need to be provided with dignity, self-respect, and pride as a foundation on which to start learning those things we need to know to live fully and productively. You helped to shape my dream. Sometimes it seems, it feels, far from reality, and I know it's not easy. I am willing to work for it, though- It is a part of me now. Thank God we were lucky enough to have ever had you as a teacher, mentor, counselor, and someone who cared for us, which is hard to find practically anywhere.

Thanks for caring and sharing.

My son, Renny Tyson, Jr. (retirement celebration June 2015)

Family, if you have ever seen anyone in her family not striving for more, it's not her fault. It's amazing how one day you retire, and the next day you can't leave your passion because you feel there is more to be done with the knowledge and experience G-d has provided to you. Mom, I love you, and I am so proud of what you have accomplished in your life! I know G-d is not done with you yet; please continue to be a beacon of light to others and your family. Thank you for all the lessons and lectures that provided direction just at the right time to help me be what G-d designed me to be. I love you. I love you. I love you.

My son, Corey Tyson (Love Letter to my mom at age 21)

I am writing to ensure that you get what I believe in my heart, that you are not only a great person, a great friend, and a wonderful mother, but you are a confirmed and convicted Christian who inspires me to be the same, along with others. You showed me that G-d has to be the leader in your life because He will let everything fall in place. Knowing that has been the most helpful in my journey to finding my manhood, to let G-d show me the way.

My son, Alan Tyson (retirement celebration June 2015)

Jeremiah 29:11-13 "For I know the plans I have for you," declares the Lord, "plans to prosper you and not to harm you, plans to give you hope and a future. Then you call upon me and pray to me, and I will listen to you. You will seek me and find me when you seek me with all your heart."

"Those words are so true, especially for my mom, because her work with teaching kids and teaching teachers can be frustrating. It can be hard. It would be best if you had faith that what you're putting in a person's mind sticks, and it would stay in there for a long time. For example, if you get stopped by a police officer, you know the right and smart thing to do. It begins with education. It began the day we were born. Education was the key, and my mom has been indefinitely blessing us to ensure that we know that until we die. She is a woman who has taught me so much about faith, determination, going after what you want, and never giving up. She taught me not only by saying it but by doing it. I loved every single minute, whippings, and teachable moments."

My Friend, Darcel Williams (42 years of friendship) (retirement celebration June 2015)

"Like Moses, who spent 40 years leading his people to the Promised Land, Linda has spent many years teaching students, adult teachers, and parents to promises of their future even when they couldn't see it or believe it for themselves. She has touched all of our lives and set the bar high for all educators around her. She makes me more thoughtful and intentional as a leader to ensure that all children are being touched and growing academically to the best of my ability. I pray that you continue pushing the envelope for equity in our children's lives.

"If you know anything about Linda, you know she loves the Lord first and foremost. She demonstrates being a child of GOD through her communication with you. You can feel her loving spirit as well as her positive energy. This is one reason why others are drawn to her. I have been blessed in so many ways, and it was Linda who reminded me that all things are possible with GOD. He was in control and not me."

My Friend, Tracey Yarbrough (37 years)

Linda is one of the most caring and generous people that I know. She once told me always to give unconditionally and not because I expect something in return.

Linda demonstrates unconditional love for her children. I was fortunate to witness this firsthand as she adopted me into her family during my college years living correction are behaviors that I have implemented to raise my children.

The best and most teachable moment is one of keeping your word. If Ms. Linda, did not keep her word to a colleague, we would have never met. Dr. Akerman told her to look after me while I was in college. Dr. Akerman gave her my name, but she didn't inform me of her or the new assignment. The college semester. Her listening ear and started, and a few months later, out of nowhere, I received a message to give this woman a call. One of the best phone calls that I ever made as I met a sista's girlfriend for life! I love you lady.

My niece, Michelle Gibson (June 2020)

Proverbs 31:26 "She opens her mouth with wisdom and the teaching of kindness is on her tongue."

"I appreciate all of our talks. You always have a life lesson for me. And always uplift me and always remind me to put my trust in G-d. Thank you for your kindness and wisdom."

My one and only daughter by grace, Ugochi, May 2020

"You breathe out encouragement, wisdom, advice, admonishment, counsel, suggestions, help to steer me towards my interests and nurture me constantly to develop me into a useful tool in the Lord's hands. You are a true beacon of light and a candle to help guide my way. You have left an indelible mark in my life, and your presence has made me a better woman, daughter, wife, mother, friend, and colleague."

Colleague and Friend, Sandra Phillips

I have known Dr. Gibson Fletcher in a professional capacity that grew to friendship. I worked with Dr. Gibson Fletcher as her Assistant Principal, and I learned so much from her that I now apply to my role as Principal. The most important lesson learned was that you should always have high expectations for all stakeholders involved, no matter the situation. Do not waiver on these expectations. As her Assistant Principal, I watched her model this over and over. It began with monitoring almost 400 students single-handedly in the cafeteria. Dr. Gibson Fletcher laid out the expectations for the students. My colleagues and I thought it could never be done.

Within two days, all students were following the expectations, and breakfast was in order. Then, she modeled how to take state testing very seriously in a school of low-performing students. In that year, 100% of the students attended every testing session. Having all students sit for a test was unheard of and uncommon. Then, the test scores were the best they had been in years. All of this was accomplished by having high expectations. As the Principal of my building, I use this as a model for my teachers, students, and families. I have high expectations of all, and it is known. Holding high expectations for everyone has earned me the respect of the district and community. I cherish every lesson learned by Dr. Gibson Fletcher, but this lesson has impacted my life tremendously, and I will be forever grateful.

My colleague, M. Gayle Burris (November 1995)

"For understanding so much about me and trusting me to know so much about you. For your sense of humor and your seriousness of purpose…For helping to build the dreams and leading me to the light at the end of the end."

My Mentee, Kristina Walters-Gowers (September 2020)

"Again, thank you for seeing something in me and encouraging me. Through this process, you have stuck with me, been my champion, and both pushed me and fought for me. Thanks for believing in me enough to make sure I accomplished this momentous achievement. I am so lucky to have been assigned you as my mentor. There are not enough words to truly express my gratitude, but I hope you will accept my heartfelt thank you as the best words I could come up with to say how much you are appreciated."

My 3rd and 5th-grade student, Eddie Moore (1983)

I am so thankful to have learned SO MANY life lessons from you;
Staying humble,
Staying calm in chaos,
The importance of education,
Making a decision and owning the outcome (i.e., handshakes, truck picture)
But the lesson learned I have decided best is maintaining your composure & dignity when you meet challenges. Which you did through the handshake and picture exchange.

References

A Framework for Understanding Poverty (Third Revision Edition, 2003), Aha! Process, Inc., P. O. Box 727, Highlands, TX 77562-0727, Website: www.ahaprocess.com

Bible: NIV

(ISRIC World Soil Information: Stephan Mantel: PO Box 353 6700 Aj Wageningen The Netherlands [+31(0)317483735])

Acknowledgments

With gratitude…

To my love and Hubby Roosevelt, Jr., who looks at me, sees my inner beauty and workings, understands me, and still loves me no matter the time of day. I finished this book because of his love; he shared it in the marketplace regarding my desire to write this book, and he found me an editor. This journey with him will hold a special place in my life and this relationship. This book will be a "stone of remembrance" about my husband, who sought to give me what I wanted and needed, and went to the streets to find it. I am eternally grateful; thus, I have sealed my love and signed it with my love stroke on the dotted line for you. Thank you!

To my three sons, Renny, Jr., Corey, and Alan Tyson, you provided the stimulus for me to write this book. It was the lessons you learned throughout your lives that sparked a desire for me to respond. I am grateful that you took time out to reflect on our time together as a family. Your written words to me were more than I could have ever hoped for from my sons. Woven throughout were expressions of love in the lessons. The tough days you experienced, the timelessness of lessons you learned, carried you through your challenges and triumphs. Most of all, the most intentional lesson of them all that showed forth in everything all of you discussed was the power of G-d. Thank you for listening and allowing me always to stop and provide a "teachable moment." You heard but not without opinion, challenges, or a need for asking for clear explanations or examples. Your honesty and love humble me and are never taken for granted. I am so grateful that G-d chose me to be your mother and friend. Finally, keep these words as stones of remembrance of nearly everything I learned and everything our Father placed inside of me to understand and share from this point. Thank you for the gift of your heart captured in the pages of this book. While my mind is sharp and I am at the pinnacle of my life, I wanted you to know my love for you and hope for all the days of your life. This document is a precious gift from me to you for you, your children, and your children's children.

Thank you, Corey; I want to say a special thank you to you for always encouraging me to write this book. Your little notes, pictures of books written, and repeatedly telling me that I could do it were instrumental in keeping my focus on my goal. I want you to know that you were right, and your encouragement charged me to "Do it!" Thank you!

To my Pastor and friend Robert Nuako for always going before the Father on my behalf, teaching me about the power of our relationship with the Most High G-d, Our Father, and the amazing love He demonstrated to us through His Son Jesus. I will be indebted to you for lifting the veil, making me aware of Our Father's unyielding grace, mercy, authority, and inheritance granted to keep me by His Love to empower me to do great things on Earth.

To my sister by grace and love, Darcel Williams, thank you for hearing my pain and joy and always making a way to be near to provide support. Your love as a sister-girlfriend is rich and irreplaceable. Together we have witnessed life lessons, the consequences, gifts, and rewards. You have helped me more than you know to come to some poignant realities about life, captured throughout the pages of this book. You have been not only a treasure to me but also to my entire family. Thank you for demonstrating love in action.

To my sister Dinnah Gibson, brother Hyman and sister- in law Connie Gibson, sister-in-law Traci Fletcher, brother and sister in-laws Anthony and Dr. Vista Fletcher, and Momma Betty James, your love and support gives my heart confidence to do and be more.

To my niece, Michelle Gibson, for always cheering me on in all of my endeavors, thank you. I am grateful for the unselfish love you give, the willingness to learn and grow, and your constant desire to be the best you can be. While you are proud of me, I am so proud of you.

To my daughter and son by grace, Ugochi and James Akoi, who adopted me as their mother/godmother/grandmother and made me a member of their family for all of my days. You make me feel unique, and your love enables me to become more of who I am and can be.

To the Matriarch of the Warren Family (Kristyn and Karlin), Allene, who adopted my entire family and treated us like we were born into the family by the late great Georgia Williams. Thank you for always remembering us and being there to support us.

To my daughters-in-law, JaQuira and Javonne Tyson, thank you for all you do to help our family be complete. Your work as a mom and wife is endearing and appreciated.

To my niece, Tasha and nephew Baldy Keeten, thank you for always showing me love and respect, opening your home to me, my family, and friends. Your kindness will forever mark a special place in my heart.

My dearest friends Latina and John Moss, Ron (Carolyn) Miller, Ken (Traci) Edwards, Deb, and Rod Woullard, Martha Miles, Betty Dye, Carrie Boston, Geri Shelton, Angela Mosley, Stacie Daniels, Tracey Yarbrough, Cynthia and Rex Mason, Art Brooks, Rosemary and Dr. Cecil Parker, Jakki (Rob) Downey, Sally (Eddie) Buxton, Janet Tribble, Valdia Burns and Ruby McNeil, Theresa and Larry Nelson, Sandra Phillips, Taffy Hunter, Sharice Thomas, Pauline Jackson, Eddie Moore, Latasha Bah and Dr. Alma Rodriguez for a fantastic life journey of love, fun, laughter, advice, tears, and joy you all provided in my life. I am a better human being because of the lessons and stories shared between us. Thank you for adding an extra heaping of love to my life.

Thanks for choosing me to be your sister and allowing me to pick you as my newfound sisters, Sheila Jones and Deb Banks. Your love and kindness have enhanced my life.

Church Ladies Extraordinaire (CLE)-Yolanda Hunter, Laura (Kevin) Rice, Christine Butler, Glendora Muldrow, and Gloria Hill, thank you for knowing the power of G-d and allowing it to grow our love, friendship, and purpose. Our relationship is a highlight of G-d's power of love.

My Amazing Kroger Crew (AKC)-Sharon Wilson, Violet,

Darnell, and Ms. Dorothy, Brent, Ms. Durella, and Voszi, thank you for making Thursday Night dinners the most fun event of the week, for sharing your lives, experiences, and friendship with me.

Affectionately my friends, the work "girls," Dr. Stacey Brinkley, Dr. Dee Morgan, and Porsche Chisley. You shared your talents and skills to help me become a better educator and improve my expertise to help all children be successful.

In loving memory of my sister-girl friend Maria Myers who demonstrated to all of us the absolute power of love and kindness. I miss her and will always keep her words of wisdom, friendship, and love deep in my heart.

To my editor, Ms. Diana, there are no words for what the Lord gave to you to give to me. Thank you for always believing in me and my message. Thank you for consistently reminding me that my voice had a meaning, purpose, and audience. I never knew that there was you, so, therefore, you had to be an angel, sent to me by way of our husbands to achieve my goal. Your keen eye touches me, the carefulness you applied to my words, the plan of action, Monday reminders, and the zoom meetings you provided to complete this project. I will never forget this life experience and how you changed my life. I will never forget that when I cried out, "The Lord a provided a ram in the bush," and it was you. Blessings to you!

About the Author

Dr. Gibson Fletcher received her Ph.D. in 2002 from the University of Dayton in Educational Leadership. She is noted for her successfully creating environments which enable students who are typically labeled "At Risk" and "Academically Challenged" to thrive because of teacher empowerment. During her tenure as a principal and superintendent, Dr. Gibson Fletcher presented extensively on Direct Instruction. She was able to structurally and statistically improve achievement scores of low-income impoverished students in buildings and districts on standardized and state test. Because of her success, she was enlisted to be the first director/principal of the Millennium Community school in 1999 and key part of her work was evaluation, hiring staff and personnel and the delineation of academic programs and training of staff because of her educational expertise and leadership ability she set a strong foundation and the school is one of two schools remaining after the opening of 26 schools in 1999.

Dr. Gibson Fletcher has worked in districts across the US with a vengeance to weed out and change the belief that students of color could not perform at the same level as their counterparts.

She's communicated and demonstrated how to seamlessly implement and correlate all programs across all disciplines. Her career in education has been as a change agent she continues to use your skills at the state level by serving on the District Review Team, in the area of Leadership and Curriculum, for The Ohio Department of Education, she is an adjunct professor for Cappella University, where she teaches principal and leadership courses.

She tutors throughout the year children in preparation for kindergarten and intervention for reading. In 2020, she wrote and published three children's books: *Get Smart, Believe, Doc's House,* and she co-authored *We Act Safely* with her husband Roosevelt Fletcher. Dr. Gibson Fletcher formed a non-profit organization in 2020 called Inspire 2 Teach 1, to ensure that vulnerable and at-risk youth populations have access to critical information and resources that could increase their opportunities in the fields of education, the arts, finance, health, and wellness. She believes that people matter, and we make a difference, and we should be the first to love and to care.